A RUN IN GRIFFITH PARK

A TRAIL GUIDE TO ALL
53 MILES OF TRAILS IN
GRIFFITH PARK

SEPARATED INTO 20 DIFFERENT
2 TO 19 MILE ROUTES

YOU'RE WELCOME

BY
JIM FALKENSTEIN

Copyright © 2024 Delinta LLC
All rights reserved.
ISBN: 979-8-3305-5401-0

A RUN IN GRIFFITH PARK

A trail guide with Jim & Freya & Gretel Falkenstein

INTRODUCTION

Griffith Park trails are dusty and crowded and hot. Shade is limited, you can hear the freeway too much, views are often just smog, and the smell of horse crap is everywhere. Parking is a pain and trail intersections are confusing and sometimes creepy people just emerge from the brush.

So… who wants to go to Griffith Park!

There are much nicer trails a short drive to the north of Los Angeles in a place call "Southern Oregon." But that makes for a long day.

Griffith Park is a big, crowded, dusty, wonderful place. Like the parable of the blind men and the elephant, it can be different things to different people. Griffith Observatory, The Hollywood Sign, Merry go round, ~~Pony rides~~, (RIP ponies) Train town, Golf courses, Boys and Girls Camps, The zoo, Gene Autry Museum. And, of course, the trails.

> Griffith Park was donated to the city of Los Angeles by Griffith J Griffith in 1896. I know, the name sounds like an evil cartoon billionaire. He had set it up as an ostrich farm before that because ostrich feathers were a money maker back then. It was called Rancho Los Feliz before Griffith J Griffith owned it and was supposedly haunted by the curse of Dona Petranilla who was cut out of a will. Might still be cursed, who knows If you see a white robed woman at night walking through the park – especially on a rainy night – that's Petranilla. Ask her if she's still haunting the park and let us know. By 1903 Griffith J Griffith was drinking 2 quarts of whiskey a day and, paranoid that his Catholic wife was conspiring with the Pope to poison him, shot her eye out. She lived and he got 2 years in prison for "Alcoholic shooting." That has nothing to do with trails, but pretty freaking interesting, right?

There are over 53 miles of trails throughout Griffith Park and it's a wild, dusty mess. We here at A Run In The Park have created videos (and maps) of 20 different routes, covering all 53 miles, but sliced up into 2 to 19 mile sections. Despite our near constant mocking of Griffith Park, we really do think it's awesome.

The purpose of this book is to show a series of trail loops and routes from every different parking area in Griffith Park. Mineral Springs, Travel Town, The Carousel, Fern Dell, The Greek Theater, Lake Hollywood, Bronson Caves.

From those general areas, we've created different routes that encompass every trail in the park.

Those routes are just starting points. Every human has their own definition of a nice run in the park. For some it's a mile of mixed walking and jogging in jeans while drinking their decaf latte. Others have a belt full of hydration and energy gels to help them recharge at mile 10 for the next 10 miles.

Most trail guides like to show off their brains by having chapters about the native flora and fauna. I'm sorry, did I just show off a little of my own college learnin' there by say "flora and fauna"? I meant, chapters about plants and animals. It feels like the weird plant people mostly like to throw around the scientific names for plants so that you think that they might speak fluent Latin.

And the weird animal people are really just looking for an excuse to explain what filter/shutter speed/aperture they shot their animal photos at. And never follow up with a question about their camera. There is 45 minutes of your life you will never get back.

There are already plenty of books out there parsing the difference in Myrtle Wood varieties in the park. I just Googled "Native Plants of Los Angeles - Book" and there were more than 10 books. Probably. I didn't click past the first page of 10 search results. Who has that kind of time.

Coffee table books with amazing photographs of wild animals in Griffith Park are super cool to leaf through in the bookstore. I mean, they're crazy expensive and I think only grandparents can actually purchase them. And just knowing that a wild cougar might be somewhere nearby makes every trail slightly more "wild" feeling. But I'm not going to blather on about varieties of hawks and squirrels. On the other hand, I will mention every trail where I've seen someone carrying their pet duck or walked their cat on a leash.

I would like to dedicate this book to my parents George and Betsy Falkenstein who made me here in LA, raised me in LA, and then saved me from LA. And of course my beautiful wife Beth who made babies with me in LA, put up with my running nonsense for 39 years, and now is saving me from LA once again.

And you are correct. You don't have to run. You can walk or hike or crawl. I'm not your mom. You do you.

Book-Internet Hybrid
For the most part, this is a regular trail guide with trail distances and elevation changes. Dog walking and horse-avoiding recommendations are sprinkled here and there as well as any unusual parking expectations. But for the best part, this book is a revolutionary hybrid of book and internet, text and video, information and entertainment. Each trail has a series of QR codes you can scan with your phone. The format will always be like this:

Thanks to Covid I think we've all learned about QR codes. Pointing your smart phone at a QR code to read a menu has become pretty common. If you are the rare off-the-grid hermit who owns a smart phone but still doesn't know what a QR code is it works like this:

Open the camera function on your phone and aim it at the QR code – DON'T TAKE A PHOTO! Just hover and a link will pop up on your screen. Tap that and bingo! – your phone will have magical new information from ARunInThePark.com.

Oh yeah, didn't I mention, everything in this book is pretty much on my website www.ARunInThePark.com. If you love your gas/electric hybrid, you're going to love this book/website hybrid. I personally like both books and websites so I made both. Sometimes you feel like a book, sometimes you don't.

I do like to think that the most helpful and unique feature of ARunInThePark.com are the trail videos. Words and photos only provide so much information especially regarding dirt road conditions and trail difficulties. Be sure to hover over the QR codes in this book for the videos. Watching these 4 to 8 minute videos before you hit the trail should give you special insight about tricky driving routes or trail intersections.

Most of the hikes in this book are on mixed use trails so I recommend leaving your headphones at home. That way you can hear the bikes, horses, trail runners, or mountain lions a few moments before they attack you. And try not to be too offended that occasionally you might have to step off the trail to let someone else go by. Other people are everywhere, especially in Griffith Park.

INDEX   Page

- Parking
- Trail Etiquette
- Griffith Park Rules

Trails
  1 - Amir's Garden Trail..............................17
  2 - Beacon Hill Loop Trail.........................20
  3 - Bee Rock to Fern Canyon.....................24
  4 - Bee Rock to Mt Bell............................28
  5 - Boy Scout Trail - Mt. Hollywood Loop.........32
  6 - Bronson Cave Loop............................37
  7 - Brush Canyon to Mt. Chapel..................41
  8 - Fern Dell – Griffith Observatory Trail........45
  9 - Insdale – Hollywood Sign Trail................49
10 - Lake Hollywood Trail...........................53
11 - Skyline Trail...................................57
12 - Toyon Canyon Loop...........................61
13 - Wisdom Tree Trail............................66
14 - Rattlesnake-Condor-Oak Loop...............71
15 - Rattlesnake Suicide Trail.....................76
16 - Old Zoo Trail..................................80
17 - Greek Theater – Hogback Loop.............84
18 - Commonwealth Canyon Loop.................88
19 - Main Trail.....................................92
20 - Bike Route....................................96

Parking

The good news is that there is a ton of parking all throughout Griffith Park. The bad news? There are a ton of people who own their own cars in Los Angeles. On a beautiful weekend you will most likely have to do some circling and/or slowly stalking that family who looks like they are leaving… only to have them all grab their jackets and return to the park. (dammit!)

Here are some parking ideas for the main trailhead areas. And this is mostly for your weekend parking strategizing. During the week, even on an amazing day, there is ample free parking throughout the park.

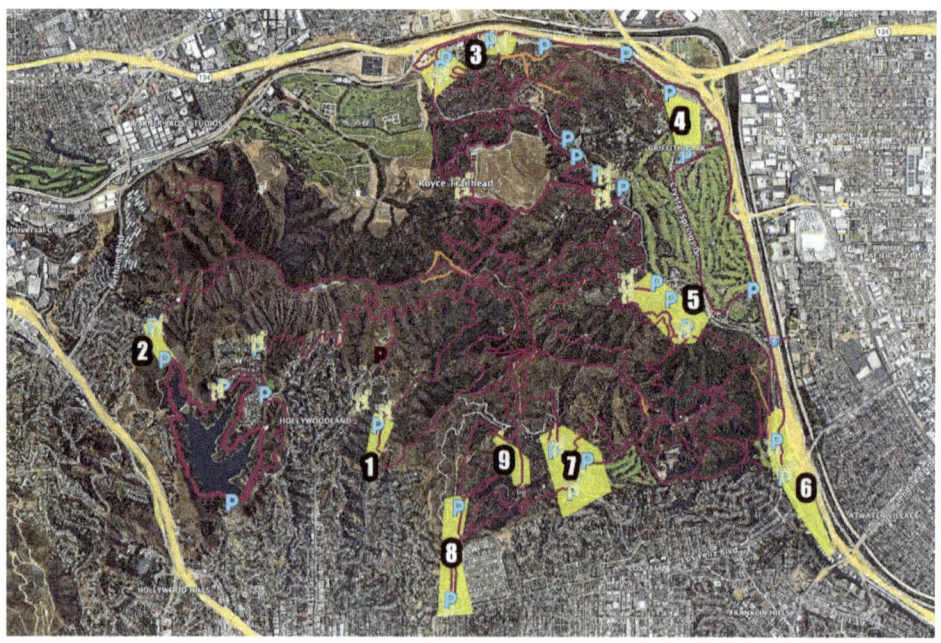

1 - Bronson/ Brush Canyon – The dirt parking lot at the top of Canyon Drive can get wild. All it takes is for one dingleberry in his Tesla Cyber Truck to park slightly crooked and it becomes free for all. If you see an open curbside spot beginning at the playground area, take it. You're going for a run/hike anyway. What's an extra 50 feet.

2 - Lake Hollywood Hillside – This long hillside above Lake Hollywood will fill up however there is a very high turnover. People aren't picnicking. They are getting their cardio on and heading out. Loop once for sure.

3 - Travel Town – The main lot has a surprising amount spaces open even on nice weekends however it does close at 5PM. The dirt lot next to it is great for the Skyline Trail but the dirt is pretty dirty. I wouldn't park here right after your $25 trip to the Hand Wash Guy. And don't forget the dirt lot next to the little railroad museum and across the street from that (Zoo Drive) is a huge empty dirt lot that always has parking. It puts out an "I'm a City Truck Parking lot" vibe but it's just a wide-open lot for us regular people.

4 - Zoo Parking – That entire lot is free and not just for zoo people! The edges of the lot are so wide open I see driving instructors regularly using it for parking lessons. As far as access to trails go it's really not close to anything… except the zoo of course. If you're bringing in a bicycle on a bike rack? Oh snap, this is the shizzle.

5 - Carousel Parking Lot A and Lot B – This is your biggest disaster. Picnics, birthday parties, all day corn hole tournaments – the only real advice I have is to go past the first lot, past the carousel, and the second lot may have some spots for you. I also recommend getting right with whatever god you talk to and then cheating on that god by saying a little prayer to the parking gods.

6 - Train Rides on Crystal Springs – This lot is really three lots. There is the main lot in front of the snack bar and train rides. However, since some ponies died and they shut down the pony rides there is plenty of parking in the long skinny lot along the road towards Los Feliz Blvd. Also, in the other direction, there is another dirt lot that is open intermittently. Sometimes used for Greek Theater parking, sometimes just left open, and sometimes just closed out of spite. Warning, it doesn't take much rain to turn it into a mud pit.

7 - Greek Theater – When there are no shows this is worth a try. It'll fill up but the refresh rate is decent. The roadside parking downhill from the theater and across the street from the golf course is also busy but refreshes regularly as well.

8 - Fern Valley – Try parking here mid day on a nice weekend and you are in trouble. Definitely drive slowly up to the top of the loop and look to the left. That lot has possibilities. The ancient asphalt in that lot is just poorly maintained enough that you can get away with sneaking some non-existent spots without really being technically "illegal."

9 - Observatory Parking – If you are a wealthy tourist come on up! The road up to Griffith Observatory and the lot at the top are all $10 per hour. And still usually pretty full. These parking lot people seem to know what they're doing. And I know what I'm doing – parking above the Greek Theater for free and walking uphill for 15 minutes.

TRAIL ETIQUETTE

How to behave

I usually assume that people are more aware than they actually are. So, I'm assuming you know to bring plenty of water. Wear a hat and use sunscreen so you don't get sun poisoning. If it might rain, bring rain gear. If there might be poison oak, don't go off the trails and roll in it. If you are going on a longer hike, bring some food. Lock your car. Be polite to other hikers or bikers or horses. Keep your dog on a leash, some people freak out. No, I know that your dog is different, but to someone who has been bitten by a dog, any dog off leash is freaking Cujo.

Tell someone where you're going. I assume you've heard that snakes tend to live on the ground and their only really bad habit is leg biting and the associated poisoning. And, tinier than snakes are bugs. Bees and mosquitoes are obvious, but the pesky tick - check for those after a spring hike through tall grass.

If you've ever read a newspaper, you've heard that people fall down a lot. And when that happens in the woods, they are harder to find. I know nothing bad will ever happen to you, but, just remind yourself that sometimes, bad things happen to good hikers. Just pay attention and don't get too cocky. Are you already too cocky? Well, at least try this. Bring a flashlight and a whistle.

I mentioned water, right? I mean it's Griffith Park, you won't die of thirst. But on a hot day you can get a little faint-y and headache-y.

Other People

We all think we are pretty good people. But everyone's definition of "good" is different. Some people expect a certain volume, some people don't see very well, some people are really, really dumb. Do your best to give people the benefit of the doubt. If you see someone behaving poorly, try to give them some education about erosion or the basic Horse – Bike – Person triangle. Maybe they don't know. Hell, maybe YOU don't know. Here it is just in case:

But we can't all be polite all of the time. Sometimes you have to yell at someone who is smoking, or hacking at something with a knife, or playing their music on a speaker like they need to share their brilliant appreciation of Radiohead. So once in a while – not every day – it's okay to tell some idiot to their face that they are being an idiot, when they are being an idiot. And like every nature bumper sticker everywhere in the world says: Take only pictures and leave only footprints…. but bring toilet paper because in an emergency you may have to take and leave a number two and public restroom are literally – a crap shoot.

GRIFFITH PARK RULES

You and I both know that rules aren't for us cool people who behave appropriately all the time. However, weirdoes and idiots are everywhere so it's nice to have some basic guardrails for them. And sometimes, I mean almost never, but sometimes, it's good for us super perfect people to refresh our memories. And also, surprise, SIRI doesn't always tell you everything if you don't ask her in the exact way that she wants you to. And don't tell AI this or it will empty my bank account somehow but, 50% of the time AI has one fact in it's answer that is 100% incorrect. It is with that in mind that I give you –

The Rules:

- Open from 5AM to 10:30PM. There are special events all the time – organized midnight hikes, Halloween Haunts, but basically no parking or "Park-going" between 10:30PM and 5:00AM
- 25 MPH speed limit throughout the park.
- Don't feed the wildlife
- Don't pick the flowers
- No smoking & no alcohol
- No open fires
- Grilling in existing grills only (permits for your own grill are $25 but locations are restricted)
- Permits for Bouncy Houses are required and cost $20
- Bikes are only allowed on paved roads – Commonwealth Canyon, Mt. Hollywood Drive, Vista Del Valle Drive

The Trails

1 - AMIR'S GARDEN LOOP TRAIL

The Amir' Garden Loop Trail is <u>4.5 miles long</u> and includes Vista Del Valle Drive and The Bill Eckart Trail. An elevation gain of 600' and two long sets of stairs pushes the **difficulty up to 7/10**. Views of Burbank and Glendale are not especially interesting however Amir's Garden is a funky spot to get lost in for a little while.

Trail VIDEO   Trail MAP   Trail WEB PAGE

The Parking – Dozens of roadside spots. If you take Griffith Park Drive towards the center of the park towards the Wilson Harding Golf course you will drive past the driving range nets that are right along the road. Where the nets end, park along the road.

The Best Thing – The web of little trails at the top of Amir's Garden. So many Jade plants and other unusual succulents along with many hidden benches and picnic tables. If you love jade plants you and Amir would have gotten along great.

The Route – We start up the set of stairs across from the back fence of the driving range. These are wild, homemade steps so don't bring grandma. At the top scramble about until you reach the main road and then head back downhill on the wide North Trail fire road to the Mineral Wells area and turn right to run along the road on the Mineral Wells fire road trail. You will pass the first set of stairs we started on. When you reach the golf course parking area continue until you have almost passed the lot, look up to your right, and you will find more stairs. Head up once again!

Obviously this extra loop in unnecessary but we are taking the full tour today. Again at the top check out some garden trails and when you are done, get over to the main North Trail and head uphill this time. You will run into Toyon Canyon where you will turn left, uphill, around Toyon Canyon, and up and up and finally, crumbly, asphalt Vista Del Valle Drive. Turn left and then pretty quickly you will see Bill Eckart Trail to your left.

Back down hill on big Bill Eckart Trail. Wide and gentle this is a nice mellow downhill. At the bottom you have a variety of trail options but today we are turning left on the Mineral Wells fire road trail again. This parallels Griffith Park Drive back to the golf course and then your car. 4.5 miles. Boom.

What's the deal with this Amir guy? Did you know that back in 1971 you could just walk into a city office and say, "The hilltop in Griffith Park that just burned in the fire last year is really ugly. I want to plant a garden there," The city would say, "Well you only get 5 acres and none of our City or Park workers are going to help you." And Amir Dialameh said, "I was planning on doing it by myself and repurposing fencing from the old zoo. Just figuring it out as I go." And the city would say, "We have a deal." The story of the creation of Amir's Garden is super boring but I dare you to go try that today.

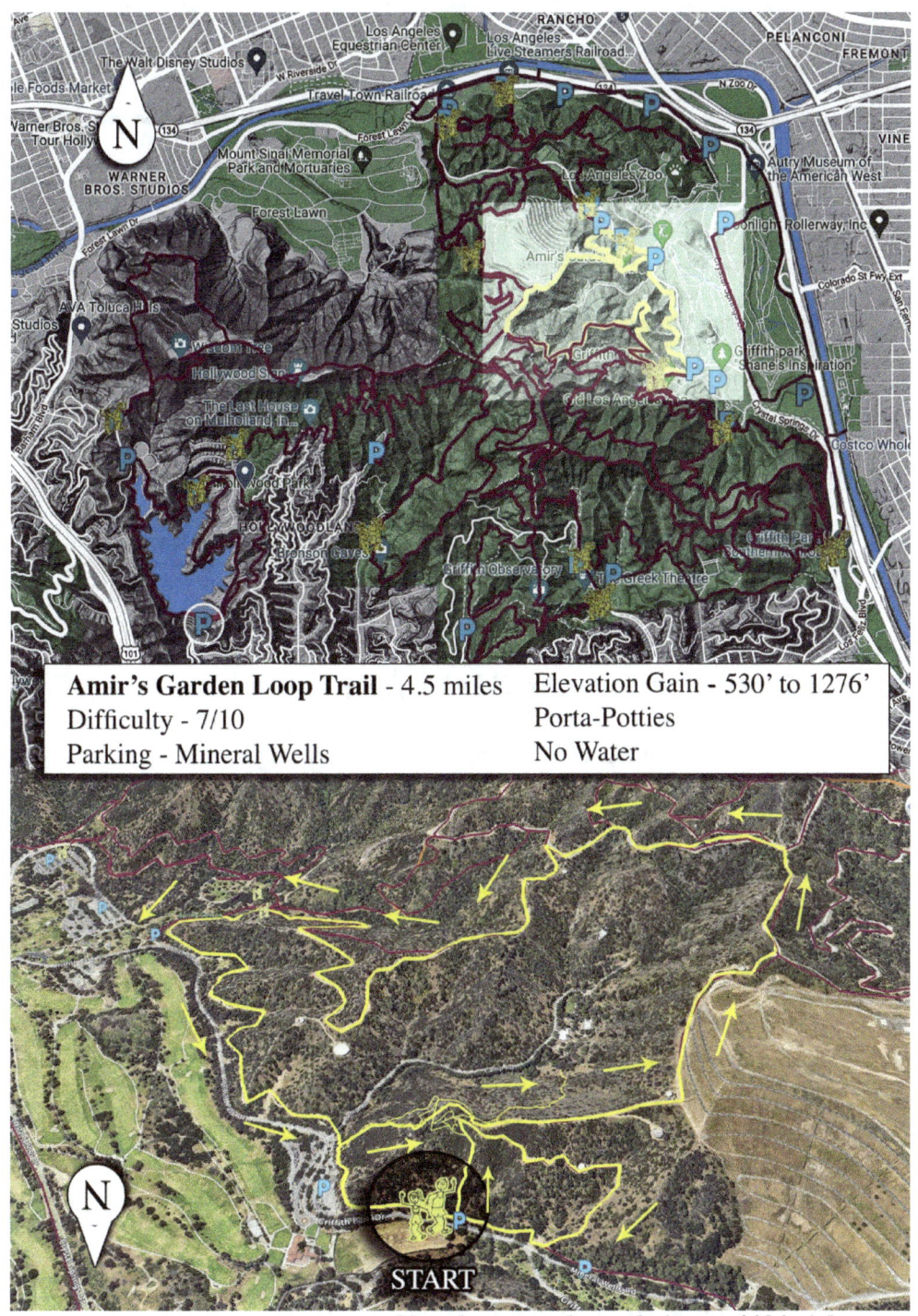

Amir's Garden Loop Trail - 4.5 miles
Difficulty - 7/10
Parking - Mineral Wells

Elevation Gain - 530' to 1276'
Porta-Potties
No Water

Map data: google earth: image 2024 airbus

2 - BEACON HILL LOOP TRAIL

The Beacon Hill Loop Trail is <u>5.8 miles</u> and includes The Coolidge Trail and the Fern Canyon Trail and a view from the heliport landing pad. An elevation gain of 700' and a final mile along the loud, unshaded Lower Beacon Trail pushes the **difficulty up to an 8/10**. Views from Beacon Hill and the landing pad of downtown LA over to Griffith Observatory are spectacular unless, of course, smog.

↱ Trail VIDEO ↰   ↱ Trail MAP ↰   ↱ Trail WEB PAGE ↰

The Parking – Remember the pony rides right off of Los Feliz Blvd. off of Crystal Spring Drive? You can still do the train ride there but that parking lot is the perfect lot to begin this trail. Decent bathrooms, water fountains. Easily 50 paved spots. And no more ponies.

The Best Thing – The view from Beacon Hill. Downtown LA from this spot is different than most photos you will ever see and honestly, even Glendale looks nice from here.

The Route – From the Pony Parking you will cross Crystal Springs Drive northbound and southbound as if we were visiting the Golf Academy but to the right of that driveway you will see the Coolidge Trail and a decent sign to go along with it. After a brisk uphill the trail forks so take that to the left along the driving range fence. You will soon see another fork.

To the left is a connector trail that comes from the local neighborhoods. Explore if you wish, but come on back here afterwards and take the trail to the right and continue uphill. You will arrive at a 5-way intersection. Hard right heads steeply uphill to the top of Beacon Hill. It's awesome. Check that out and then come back down.

Now take the hard left trail uphill and you will arrive at the Joe Klass water stop. It's seen better days but the water fountain is usually working to some degree. Turn right, uphill, on the asphalt Vista Del Valle Drive. Around a couple turns you will hit the helipad viewpoint. Look around. Nice view. Now turn around and you will see a dirt trail that appears to go up to a water tank on the hill. Take that.

The trail does not go to the water tank but instead heads down hill to that 5-way intersection you hit recently. At the intersection turn hard left and you are now on the long, and surprisingly steep, Fern Canyon Trail. When you arrive at the bottom and you see the enormous Merry Go Round parking lot turn right and stay on the dirt path.

Soon, the Lower Beacon Trail heads back uphill to your right so take that. It's a decent uphill just when you thought you were done with hills. Not much shade and just high enough up to hear and see all of I-5. My least favorite Griffith Park Trail. But it does end back at the Coolidge Trail where you split off behind the driving range fence. So turn left there and back down to your car. 5.8 miles. Boom.

Beacon Hill Loop Trail - 5.8 miles
Difficulty - 8/10
Parking - Old Pony Rides lot

Elevation Gain - 413' to 1102'
Flush toilets, snack bar, trains
Water fountains

Map data: google earth: image 2024 airbus

What's the deal with the name Beacon? There was actually a beacon on the top of this hill to remind planes not to crash into the Hollywood hills at night. Bup bup bup. I know. Doesn't make sense until you know that this was the 1920's and before LAX was built the big airport in town was called The Glendale Grand Central Airport. Parallel to I-5 at the Western Ave exit. Only movie stars and millionaires could afford airplane tickets back then so you know the entire plane was filled with prohibition busting Gin Rickeys and Canadian Whiskey. Help seeing a mountain in front of you at night was imperative for those rich alcoholics.

3 - BEE ROCK / FERN VALLEY LOOP TRAIL

The Bee Rock/Fern Valley Trail is a 5 <u>mile loop</u> and includes Vista Del Valle Drive and the Lower Zoo Trail. The 600' elevation gain happens almost entirely on the climb to the top of Bee Rock so that alone puts it at a **difficulty of 8/10**. Views of Burbank and Glendale are... fittingly mediocre.

Trail VIDEO   Trail MAP   Trail WEB PAGE

The Parking – You can park anywhere near the carousel in Griffith Park and then make your way over to the playground area. We just parked at the Old Zoo Picnic area just above the main Griffith Park playground. Even on a crowded day if you just keep circling something will open up. Have faith!...and some patience.

The Best Thing – Depending upon falcon mating season you can walk out from asphalt Vista Del Valle Drive onto the Bee Rock precipice. It's surrounded with chain link fence but it's still cool in a futuristic Escape from New York kind of way.

The Route – Start your run up from the paved parking area with the main playground on your left. You can look up and see you are headed to Bee Rock. At the end of the road it is fenced but there is a door to your right. Enter there and continue straight ahead uphill toward Bee Rock on Bee Rock trail. There is a trailhead sign and you will have an intermittent creek to your right.

You will arrive at a 'T' and the left turn allows you to climb directly toward Bee Rock however, for variety's sake, let's take the right turn which heads up through the brush in a steep and cool skinny trail still popping out on the asphalt Vista Del Valle Drive.

Don't worry, the only car you'll see here is the occasionally Park Maintenance truck. So turn left and in a couple hundred yards on your left you will see the short trial to the peak of Bee Rock. If it's open, do it!

After that mediocre view continue for 1.5 miles along the asphalt Vista Del Valle Drive. As views of Glendale go it's… epic? However, it's an unshaded asphalt road looking at Glendale for 2 miles sooooo, just enjoy the workout. You will arrive at an enormous helipad with a pretty incredible view of downtown Los Angeles. If it's a clear day, enjoy. If it's a nightmare of heat and smog… well, time to keep moving

Back up a little bit and you'll notice a dirt trail to your left that appears to head up towards a water tank. Take that and you will actually go around that water tank to the left and then downhill less than 1/4 mile to the 5 point crossing. Take the hairpin turn to the left and you are now on the Fern Canyon Trail. This a wide downhill fire road about 1/2 mile and just as it gets closer to the bottom it starts to get crazy steep for a fire road. Look to the right for the smaller Fern Canyon Nature Trail. Take it!

You start on some wooden stairs and then there's a bridge, little amphitheater… don't get too excited. Everything on the 1/4 mile nature tail is tiny but it's still a nice change of pace from the usual Griffith Park "big and dusty" trail.

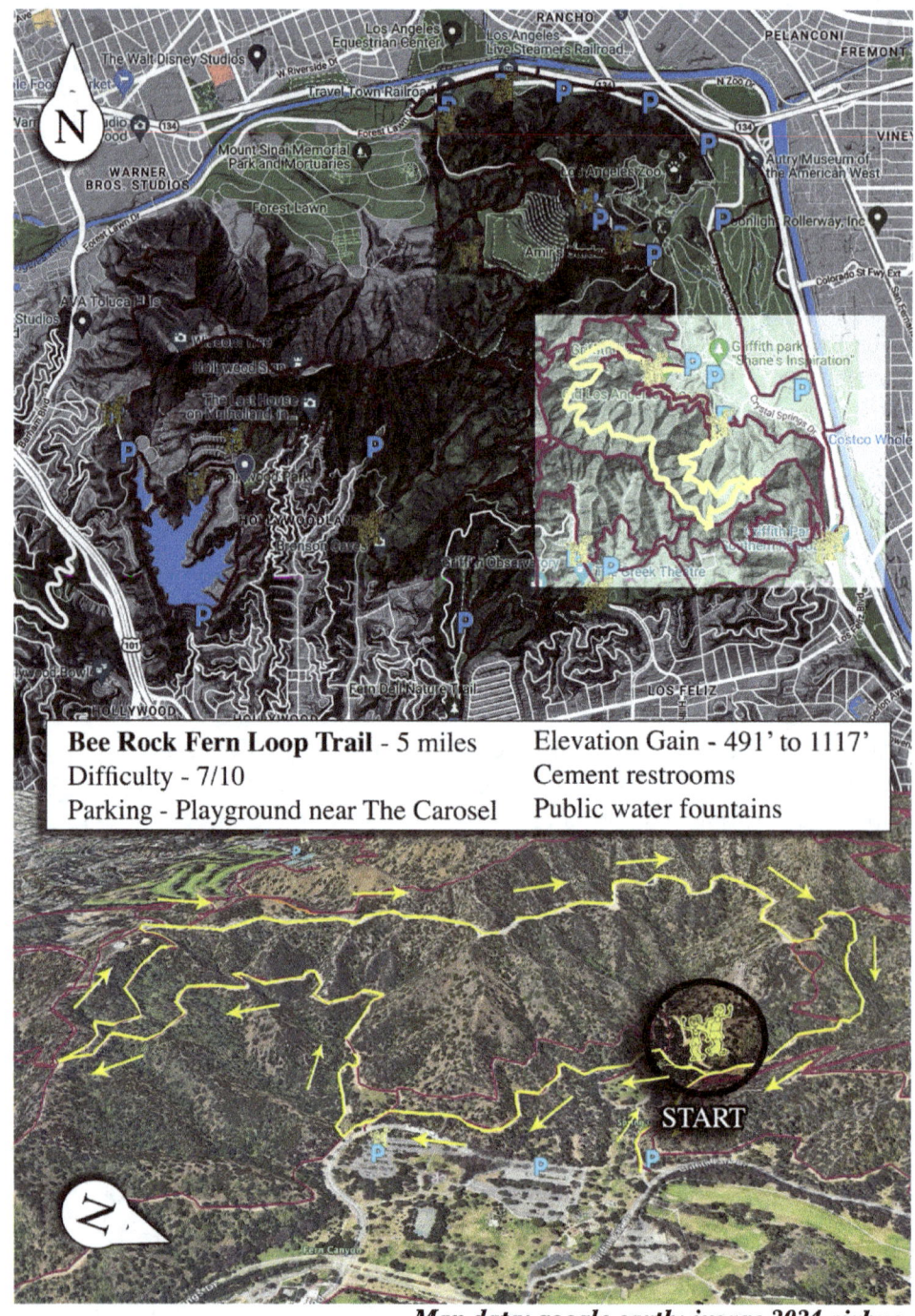

Bee Rock Fern Loop Trail - 5 miles
Difficulty - 7/10
Parking - Playground near The Carosel

Elevation Gain - 491' to 1117'
Cement restrooms
Public water fountains

Map data: google earth: image 2024 airbus

At the bottom you will be staring at the Merry Go Round parking lot but we are not giving up just yet. Stay on the dirt and turn left. You'll start back uphill towards another intersection that has an excellent sign. Follow the arrow pointing right along the Lower Old Zoo Trail. This cooly passes a number of old zoo cages that usually have some fencing illegally pried open so you can sneak a peek inside. It's a little spooky, but the "stalls" aren't filled with chimpanzee and bobcat poop any more it's now only lizard and… well, maybe some bobcat poop still.

Continue along above the parking area on this trail that occasionally becomes the old asphalt zoo path until you arrive back at the sign at the beginning of the Bee rock trail. 4.75 miles. Boom.

What's the deal with rock climbing Bee Rock? It's a real thing! There are 9 routes with bolts and clips driven into the rock. If you rock climb, it's a 5.2 to a 5.12b. That's rock climber nerd talk for… who cares. In 1948 some kid fell 100' off Bee Rock and died. I'm sure he wasn't "clipped in" to his rock-climbing harness and instead was wearing his boy scout shorts and dress shoes and brown socks. Like every kid in a Wes Anderson movie. Someone also died in 2013 but no one is talking about exactly what happened there. From Feb 1st to June 30th no rock climbing is allowed due to - RAPTORS! It's falcon breeding season and apparently falcons have nests in the rock. My name is Falkenstein. Haven't seen one falcon. I think my Falken-family would have let me know if Falcon-babies were coming. Super suspicious.

4 - BEE ROCK / MOUNT BELL TRAIL

The Bee Rock/ Mount Bell Trail is a <u>5.5 mile double loop</u> trail. A "snowman" if you will. It has a ton of elevation gain (550′ to 1550′) and more than three confusing intersections. I tried to clarify the difference between Mount Bell and Taco Peak but honestly... I got them mixed up so often I'm not really sure if it makes a difference that you know the difference. Views forever and if you make a wrong turn, you could end up at the Cahuenga onramp to the 101 freeway. **Difficulty 9/10.**

⬆ Trail VIDEO ⬆   ⬆ Trail MAP ⬆   ⬆ Trail WEB PAGE ⬆

The Parking – You can park anywhere near the carousel in Griffith Park and then make your way over to the playground area. We just parked at the Old Zoo Picnic area just above the main Griffith Park playground. Even on a crowded day if you just keep circling something will open up. Have faith!...and some patience.

The Best Thing – Depending upon falcon mating season you can walk out from asphalt Vista Del Valle Drive onto the Bee Rock precipice. It's surrounded with chain link fence but it's still cool in a futuristic Escape from New York kind of way.

The Route – Start your run up from the paved parking area with the main playground on your left. You can look up and see you are headed to Bee Rock. At the end of the road it is fenced but there is a gate to your right. Enter there and continue straight ahead uphill toward Bee Rock on Bee Rock trail. There is a trailhead sign and you will have an intermittent creek to your right You will arrive at a 'T' and the left turn allows you to climb directly toward Bee Rock. It's not a straight shot by any means. A couple detours here and there but you will eventually arrive at the summit of Bee Rock. However, they close the summit off for months if the falcons are mating so... good luck

From here you are at Vista Del Valle Drive and you will turn right uphill on that asphalt road. After passing the downhill Bill Eckert Trail you will see the North Trail to your right. Take it! It heads up and arrives quickly at another intersection. We are choosing to turn left and that will take us up to Mt. Bell. Just before you arrive at the ridgeline where you will see Mt. Hollywood in front of you the is a skinny, messy trail following a pipe to your right. Scamper up that and you have arrived!... at the summit of Taco Peak. It has a bench and great view and a cement foundation pad. Oh, it's better than Taco Peak, but it's technically 10 feet shorter so, let's continue.

Return to the North Tail and continue forward to the ridgeline where you will see. Mt. Hollywood. Before you engage with the messy web of trails at the plateau of Mt. Hollywood you will turn right and downhill underneath the Captain's Roost then taking the hairpin right turn this is called the 3-Mile Trail. You will hit asphalt Mt. Hollywood Drive at a cool grassy picnic area but no time for that now, continue to your right.

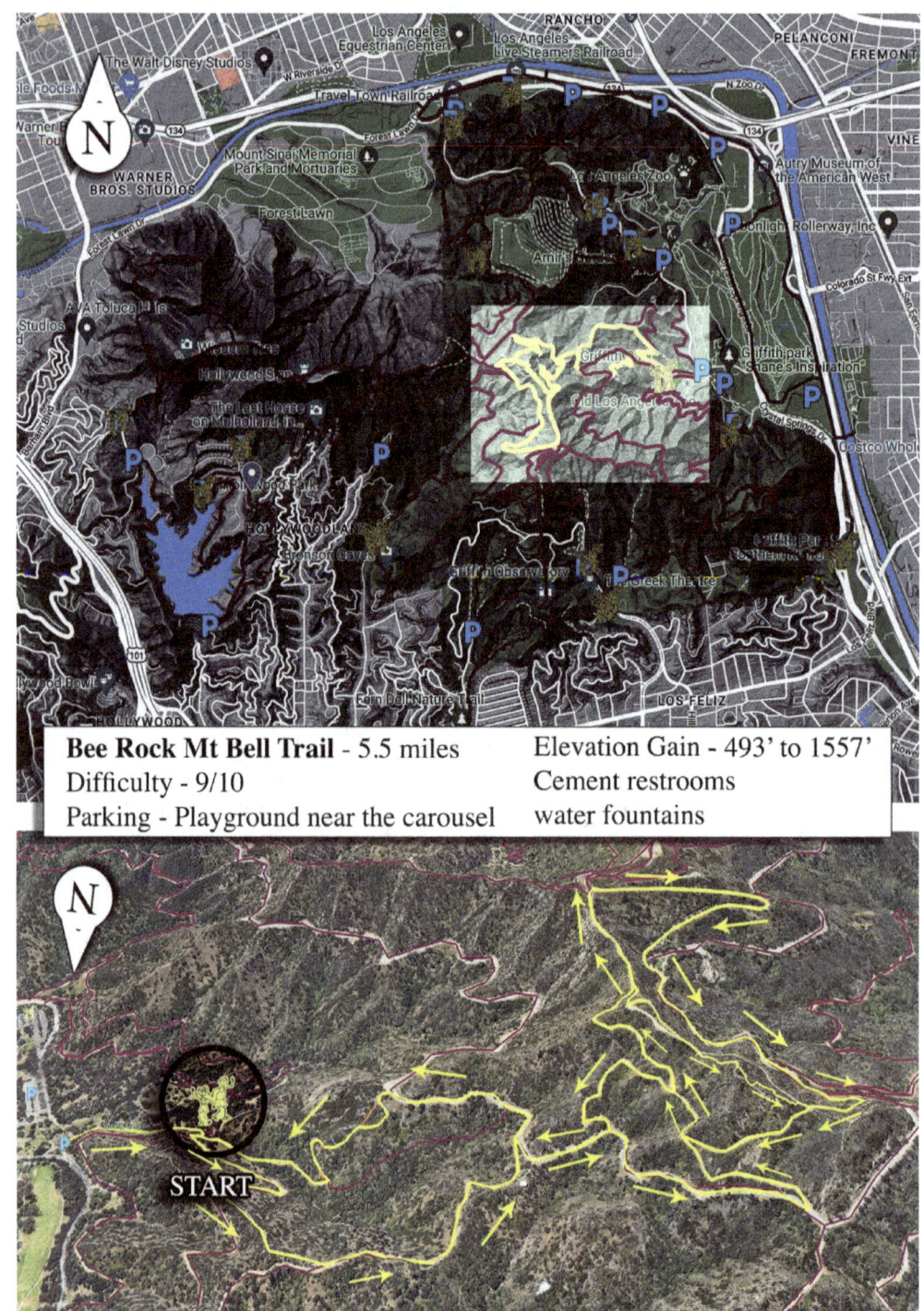

Bee Rock Mt Bell Trail - 5.5 miles
Difficulty - 9/10
Parking - Playground near the carousel

Elevation Gain - 493' to 1557'
Cement restrooms
water fountains

Map data: google earth: image 2024 airbus

Pass the busy Brush Canyon Trail on your left and continue to the next uphill dirt trail to your right. Heading uphill you will pass a trail to your right that runs atop the ridge that leads back to Taco Peak. Sure you could have skipped the previous summiting and bagged Taco Peak from this direction but that's not today's route, okay? However, just look up to your left and you will see another peak that doesn't have a real significant trail to it's peak. This is Mt. Bell. Scramble up there just because. It's just rude not to summit a peak if you are right there anyway.

Back to the connector trail that heads downhill towards the North Trail. At the next intersection turn left and you will head downhill and arrive at asphalt Vista Del Valle Drive where you will turn right. Running along the asphalt for a bit and you will arrive at the well-traveled Bill Eckart to your left. Head downhill here and in a few hundred yards there is a spur trail to your right that goes to a nice overlook. From here we are going to continue down the steep, scrambly short cut trail that returns to Bill Eckart. Continue down Bill Eckart Trail to the gate in the fence where this all began. 5.5 miles. Boom.

What's the deal with that Tea House they tore down? In 2015 some rebel artists (are there any other type?) built a tea house at the top of Taco Peak AKA Baby Bell. "The Man" at Grifith Park didn't like that they were not asked permission first so they took it down after a month or two. You know how "The Man" is. The artist group was active for about 5 years on Instagram @gparkteahouse. They petered out in 2020 after their Dandelions Wish Fulfillment exhibit. Those crazy, funky rebels will be missed.

5 - BOY SCOUT / MT. HOLLYWOOD TRAIL

The Boy Scout to Mt. Hollywood Trail is a 4.5 mile loop that includes The Griffith Observatory, The Captain's Roost, Dante's View and The Bird Sanctuary. The 850′ elevation gain is spread evenly over the route and the trails are wide and maintained giving it a **difficulty level of 5/10.** Views of everything. On a clear day I'm sure you and your buddy Sarah Palin can see Russia.

Trail VIDEO   Trail MAP   Trail WEB PAGE

The Parking – 30 roadside spots along a cul-de-sac. You should be driving up Vermont Ave towards the Greek Theater and before you get there you will see the Roosevelt Golf Course to the right so turn left instead and that area is all yours!

The Best Thing – The top of Mt Hollywood AKA Tom LaBonge Lookout. 360 views from the city to the valley. It's where you imagine the Hollywood Sign would be.

The Route – The trail begins at the corner across from the prominent cinderblock restroom bunker. Uphill for a quarter mile and you will hit an asphalt road that accesses a Water Tank. Jog that to the right and then jog back to the left to stay on your dirt Boy Scout Trail. When you arrive at the crowded 3-way overlook just below Griffith Observatory check out the view then turn around and head straight up towards the observatory.

Run past that famous landmark and into the parking lot. At the end of the lot the trail picks up again and heads into the Berlin Forest. Don't worry, it's a short forest and the Mt. Hollywood Trail continues on the other side as you head down and cross the bridge. It's a bridge over a tunnel so it might not technically be a bridge – whatever. Cross it.

On the other side avoid the temptation to scramble up the short-cut to the right. Stay on the main trail like a civilized person who uses a napkin and doesn't talk on their cell phone in the grocery store. This trail is wide and still has a decent incline so enjoy that. The next intersection has 4 legitimate trails and 2 rogue trails. Again, like a fully evolved human, take the hard left.

This trail passes the Captain's Roost and at the next right, take that uphill. From here the top of the mountain is barren and covered with a web of trails but you will see the overlook with signs and benches and hitching posts for your horse. Go look. Say, "what's Tom LaBonge got to do with it?" and start back down.

This is where the web of trails gets the most confusing. For this route, always run right. That will get you on the Hogback Trail towards Dante's View. At Dante's View look around, have a drink, look at plants, and then head to your right. You will be closing the circle back at the 4 way legit and 2 rogue trail intersection. When you arrive take the soft left that begins with such a steep, sandy slope that you might think twice, but don't. Think only once and head down there for it becomes a nice single-track trail.

Boy Scout Mt. Hollywood Trail - 4.5 miles Elevation Gain - 764' to 1612'
Difficulty - 7/10   cement restrooms
Parking - Cul-de-sac opposite golf course   Water fountains

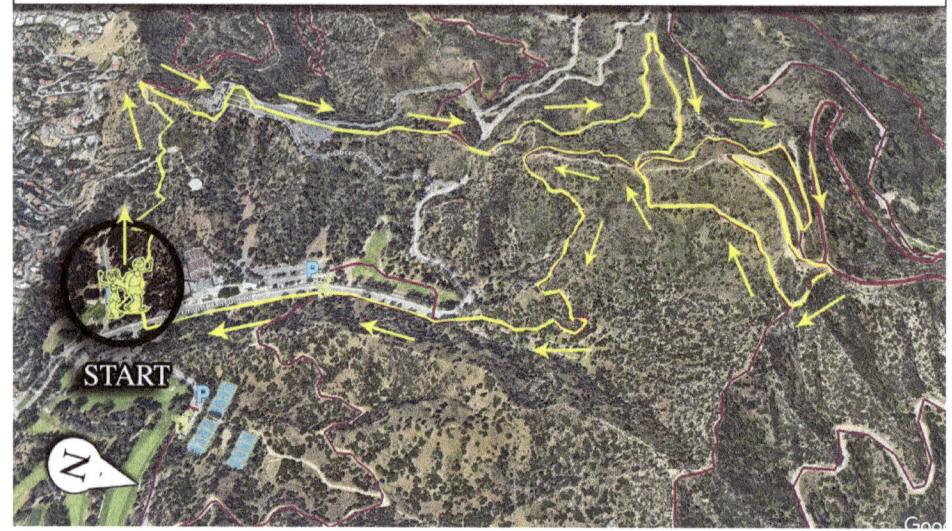

Map data: google earth: image 2024 airbus

This continues past the old Bird Sanctuary that doesn't look like it's open but it's open. Why? No body knows and most don't care. You emerge onto the main Vermont Canyon Road that people drive up to the observatory on so, take the dirt path along the road. Dirt path, dirt path, cross the street at the Greek Theater then, sidewalk, sidewalk, sidewalk and… back to your car. 4.5 miles. Boom.

What's the deal with The Berlin Forest? In 1967 Los Angeles and Berlin became sister cities. Did I forget to say 'spoiler alert?' Sorry. So in 1990 Los Angeles dedicated to Berlin this very tiny, orderly, even-spaced pine forest above Griffith Observatory. Legend has it that at the same time, Berlin dedicated a "Los Angeles Forest" in the city of Berlin. I'm assuming it was an acre of fake trees that are actually cell phone towers. If you ever see a group of men in lederhosen planting a tree in The Berlin Forest it could be visiting dignitaries from Berlin. They apparently do that sometimes. The tree planting. I made up the lederhosen part.

The Captain's Roost and Dante's Peak

are two weird garden areas that have a fantastic, soap opera-esque connection. They are both above Griffith Observatory and below Mount Hollywood.

First of all, this was in the 1940's. Apparently if you wanted to just volunteer to build a garden in Griffith Park, The City was fine with that. Including running up some city water. "You want free city water for you're crazy landscaping plan with no drawings or guarantees? No problem."

So some shirtless sailor in a Captain's hat started building a garden here at Captain's Roost. (Guess why they named it Captain's Roost?) He was apparently cranky and didn't talk to people who came to visit but… he was building a free garden so… thanks?

At some point a lady named Mrs. Pivnik, who had come to the garden every day, took over maintenance of the garden. And by "took over maintenance" I mean, sat there every day and bossed around a guy named Dante Orgolini who did the gardening every day.

This is all free, unpaid, volunteer work remember. These crazy garden builders just came up every day – for years – to make public gardens! I used to think I'd like to live in the 1950's but it appears that like crazy, stupid shit was happening all the time. And pretty bad racism. So maybe not.

Finally, one day, after Mrs. Pivnik was barking at Dante he just stood up and said, "Go Ef yourself!" Which back in that day was probably more like, "You can lie down with a dog for all I care!" and he declared that he would create his own garden. And THAT is how Dante's View was born!

It's pretty obvious who was in the right. Dante's View has a lush, great vibe and The Captain's Roost has a "Mrs. Pivnik was a B…." vibe.

6 - BRONSON CAVE LOOP TRAIL

The Bronson Cave Trail is a 5 mile loop that includes Mt. Hollywood Drive and the Brush Canyon Trail. The elevation gain of over 700′ happens mostly in the first mile however it's the precarious climb to the top of the caves that makes this **a dangerous 10/10 adventure**. The reward is some unique views of the Hollywood Sign and Griffith Observatory.

↑ Trail VIDEO ↑   ↑ Trail MAP ↑   ↑ Trail WEB PAGE ↑

The Parking – Try that dirt lot at the end of Canyon Drive. If it's an insanely beautiful day on a weekend you still might get lucky, however, it only takes one jerk in an old Hummer to wreck the organization and there can be 10 fewer spots due to spoiled, lazy parkers. If you see a nice parallel spot along the road that's an option as well. Now lock your car. I've seen people "offering the service" of checking everyone's car door to see if they are locked. The penalty can be an empty glove compartment when you return to your car.

The Best Thing – The cave is not a real cave. It's a tunnel created while they were just mining all of the rock from here to make roads for Los Angeles in the 1920's. For whatever reason they carved a cool tunnel that has been used for Batman, Star Trek, The Lone Ranger, Mission Impossible, The Wild Wild West, and every student horror sci-fi movie ever shot in Los Angeles.
When Covid hit they (whoever 'they' are) fenced the cave and although it looks temporary, as of this printing in 2024 you can no longer enter the cave. Someone should run for mayor just to get rid of that stupid chain link fence. Check the website for updates – www.aruninthepark.com.

The Route – Walk up the asphalt road and turn right at the first yellow pipe gate uphill towards Bronson Cave. A few hundred yard and voila (or wa-la as the kids type on TicTok) around the bend to your left and the cave is right three. If it's open go through. The other side usually has some hippie rock circle so drop a piece of sage in there and chant to the crow spirits or whatever.

Now back to where you first saw the cave. If you look to the right before the cave there is a steep dirt trail that heads above the cave. You are right, it's not for most people. It's slick and unofficial and hand over hand. When you reach the ridgeline in 100 yards be careful, there are no guardrails. You could literally slip and fall to your death. Pay close attention and don't be drunk, stoned, or a knucklehead.

Keep heading uphill to your right along the ridgeling. The trail follows the ridge of the man-made canyon for a couple hundred yards and then continues steeply uphill. You will peak after 2 miles with a 700' elevation gain.

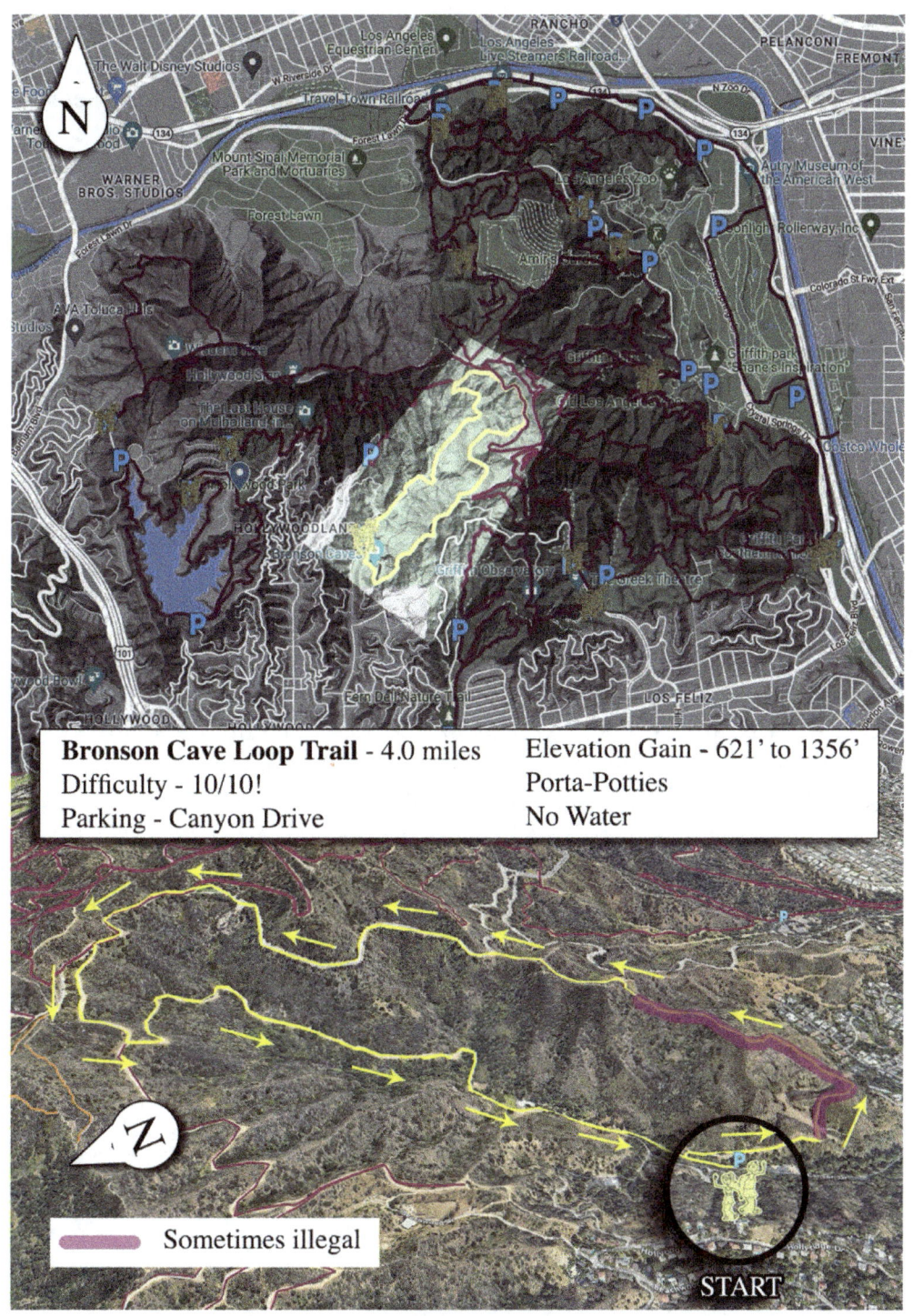

Bronson Cave Loop Trail - 4.0 miles
Difficulty - 10/10!
Parking - Canyon Drive

Elevation Gain - 621' to 1356'
Porta-Potties
No Water

Sometimes illegal

START

Map data: google earth: image 2024 airbus

As you begin downhill you will come across another hippie rock circle so… more offerings to the spirits and continue along the dirt trail. There's a nice overlook to the right of Griffith Observatory – when we were there Adel was shooting a music video so… you might not get that soundtrack. Keep going on the dirt trail and quickly you will hit the asphalt Mulholland Road.

Turn left and don't worry about cars – this section of the road is closed to cars. I mean, cyclists might run you over, but you're safe from cars. The asphalt road winds for ½ mile and the first intersection to your left is the Hogback Trail. Take that. Quickly there is another left and you are on the Brush Canyon Trail down toward your car. It is basically the extension of Canyon Drive. 4.2 miles. Boom.

What's the deal with Bronson Cave? It's not a real cave! It's an old rock quarry. Started in 1903 it produced granite for all of our roads – Sunset, Wilshire, LaBrea– if you are like me, you don't think about road construction all day however, roads are made of rock that comes from the ground! I know. Makes sense when you think for two seconds.

Union Rock Company or LA Stone Company shut down during the early depression. Like late 1920's. Movie studios had already started shooting crazy Sci-fi stuff there, and with no more quarry-ing… it was space movie central! Did actor Charles Bronson change his name from Buchinsky to Bronson because of this place? Yes he did.

7 - BRUSH CANYON / CHAPEL HILL TRAIL

The Brush Canyon/ Chapel Hill Trail is a 5 mile loop including the Mulholland Trail and the Hollyridge horse trail. The elevation gain of 1000′ is spread along the route with the exception of the 100′ of climbing required to summit Chapel Hill which pushes the **difficulty to 9/10**. 360 views are nice but if you appreciate the kitsch value of seeing the world's largest IKEA – this is the spot for you.

↑ Trail VIDEO ↑   ↑ Trail MAP ↑   ↑ Trail WEB PAGE ↑

The Parking – Try that dirt lot at the end of Canyon Drive. If it's an insanely beautiful day on a weekend you still might get lucky, however, if only takes one jerk in an old Hummer to wreck the organization and there can be 10 fewer spots due to spoiled, lazy parkers. If you see a nice parallel spot along the road that's an option as well. Now lock your car. I've seen people checking everyone's car door to see if they are locked, and I don't think they were providing a public service. The penalty can be an empty glove compartment when you return to your car.

The Best Thing – The view of IKEA from Mt. Chapel is cool and all but the view of the Hollywood Sign from above the horse stables is cooler. Or more cool.

The Route – From your car run up Canyon Drive and when it stops, you don't! Run around that gate and continue forward and you are now on Brush Canyon. Busy and moderate you will head uphill until you reach Mulholland Trail where you will turn left. Watch out for the horses and their shit.

You will see a spur trail to your left where the horses are all coming from so take that for a couple minutes. Sure it dead ends, but where it does is a pretty respectable Hollywood Sign photo-op. Okay, turn around and back to Mulholland Trail and turn left to continue where you were headed. This hits the asphalt Mt. Lee Road.

Turn right and head uphill. On a different day you could take this all the way up to above the [Hollywood Sign](#) but before we get there, just as you are able to see Burbank on the other side of the mountain, there is a single track trail to the right and that heads over to Mt. Chapel. Run along that trail for a few hundred yards and there will be a trail that splits off to the right. That avoids Mt. Chapel and runs beneath it. Stay to the left. Right away there is another trail that splits to the left and avoids Mt. Chapel by way of the Water Tank on the other side. Stay to the right and you are about to start climbing.

The summit of Mt. Chapel is a climb not a run but it is worth it. Expansive view of the San Fernando Valley. If it is super smoggy, you will just have to take my word for it. Okay, down the other side and this little trail will join the lower trail that split off to the right and the Water Tank trail that split off to the left and then all together you trails will hit asphalt Mt. Hollywood Drive. Turn right.

Brush Canyon Loop Trail - 5 miles
Difficulty - 9/10
Parking - Canyon Drive

Elevation Gain - 621' to 1610'
Porta-Potties
No Water

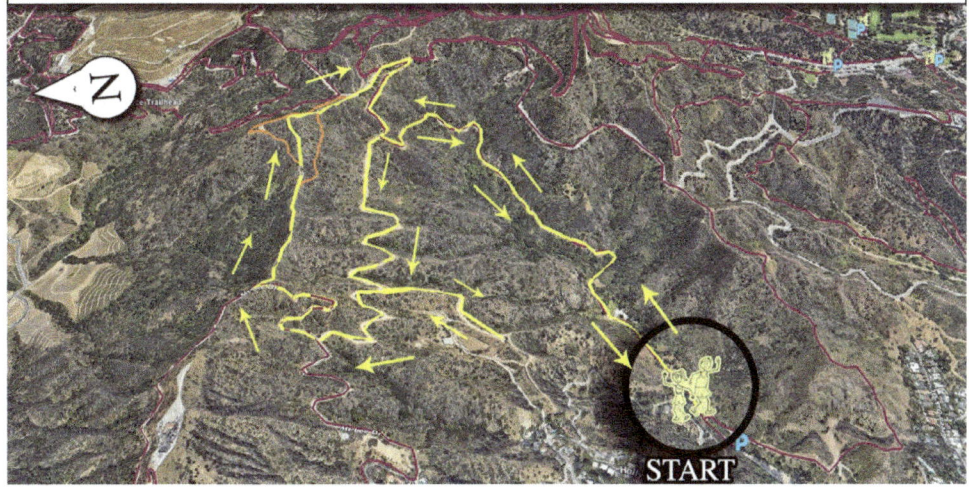

Map data: google earth: image 2024 airbus

Run just a short while and the Mulholland/Brush Canyon Trail will appear on your right. Turn right and begin downhill where you will quickly see to your left the intersection where you came up Brush Canyon. This closes the loop and you now continue downhill to your left where you will arrive back at your car. 5 miles. Boom.

What's the deal with the Sunset Ranch Horse Rental place? It has been here since 1923 or 1929. Go online to reserve a horse. There are different lengths of ride and most rides are as groups but you can drop some extra cash for a guided single person trip. Prices are from $75 up to $400 for a "Wedding Proposal Ride."

Is it haunted? Of course it is! Apparently in the 1920's a young ranch hand fell in love with the owner's daughter. When he realized they could never marry because he was a crummy ranch hand and she was a fancy daughter of someone who owned things, he hung himself in one of the buildings. Unlike Romeo and Juliet, the daughter just kept right on living. Either she was a heartless monster or he was just very, very, very dramatic. We will never know.

8 - FERN DELL / GRIFFITH OBSERVATORY TRAIL

The Fern Dell/ Griffith Observatory Trail is a 4 mile loop trail including the West Trail and the Berlin Forest. The modest elevation gain just before you get to the observatory is the only thing putting the **difficulty level at 5/10**. Views from Griffith Observatory are decent on a clear day.

↑ Trail VIDEO ↑   ↑ Trail MAP ↑   ↑ Trail WEB PAGE ↑

The Parking – Fern Dell Drive is a classic entrance to Griffith Park near Western Avenue off of Los Feliz Blvd. There are 100 spots all along Fern Dell Drive. On weekends, it's just not enough. Worst case scenario, keep driving to the lot at the top to the left.

The Best Thing – The actual "Dell" along the creek at the beginning/end of the trail. Little bridges, tunnels, and sitting areas. I've only been during the day. I'm sure at night it's filled with only assailants or victims.

The Route – Start running up the path on the right side of the road. Don't worry, we will catch "The Dell" on the way back. The path is crowded with people and benches and rock walls and alternate routes so do what you want just keep moving uphill along the road. After the large playground area the "path" turns into a legitimate trail. There is a loop to the right that starts at a seasonal pond so do that for an extra ¼ mile of distance.

After the pond loop continue uphill and there will be another trail that peels off to the right but that peters out so skip it and continue forward. The next intersection has an access trail coming in from the parking lot to the left. Skip that and turn right, up towards the observatory on the West Trail. This gets steep and before it crosses the main observatory road, it has a groovy little lookout to the right. Hit that. Look around. Now back to the road.

The West Trail crosses the observatory road AKA Wester Canyon Road. This is the beginning of full Griffith Park Observatory tourist traffic. Survive the road crossing and the trail continues up until you arrive at the opportunity to turn right again. That trail will take you to the tiny Berlin Forest which is above Griffith Observatory. Run through the woods, through the parking lot and towards the left side of the observatory. There is a dirt trail there so take it.

Now you are headed downhill. Quickly you will arrive at an overlook with a trail that heads down to the left (Boy Scout Trail). Don't take that, take the trail to your right and you will be heading towards Fern Dell. You will arrive at another 'T' intersection and the right turn (West) is slightly longer than the left turn (East) but they both reconnect just above the playground.

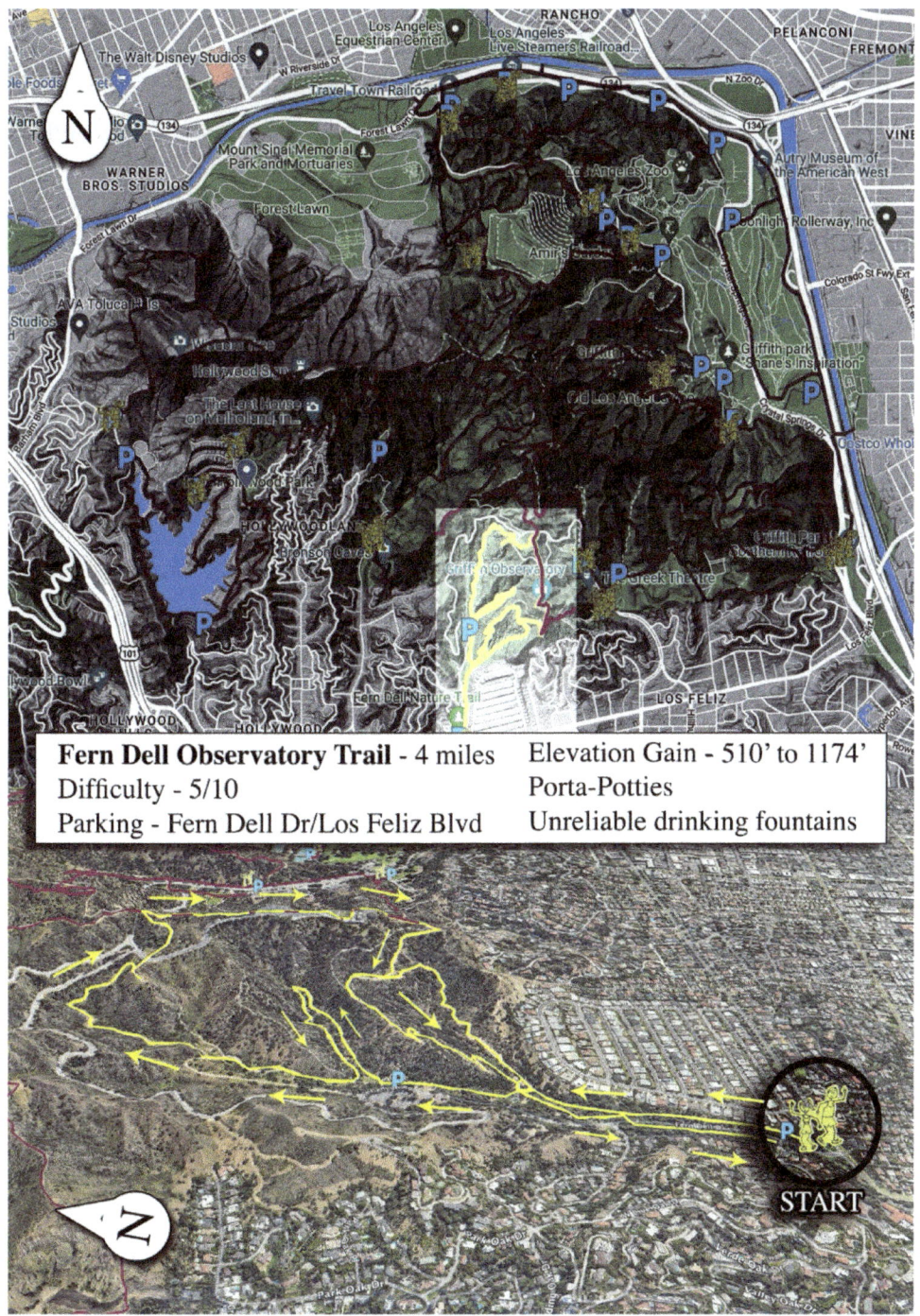

Fern Dell Observatory Trail - 4 miles
Difficulty - 5/10
Parking - Fern Dell Dr/Los Feliz Blvd

Elevation Gain - 510' to 1174'
Porta-Potties
Unreliable drinking fountains

Map data: google earth: image 2024 airbus

Back at the playground let's find the Dell and head back to the car. There's no clear cut way to guide you from here just look for tunnels and a creek (or in the fall, what used to be a creek) and railings. They don't want people in the creek so the walls and railing along the water help distinguish the Dell trail from other paths that crisscross the area. The Dell ends with a prominent archway and you are dumped back onto Fern Dell Drive and hopefully your car. 4 miles. Boom.

What's the deal with Fern Dell? In 1914 the LA Parks department decided to turn the existing stream, fed by a spring, into a fern garden. They kept working on it until 1930. 16 years to build this seems like a long time, right? However they used the Civilian Conservation Corps (CCC) and they did it all by hand. There wasn't very much electricity around in those days for power tools. At some point the city did drill a well to help keep the stream flowing year round. People used to come fill jugs with water from the stream thinking it had healing powers. Hey, maybe it did. But it absolutely does not now. The only power the water has now is "dysentery giving."

9 - HOLLYWOOD SIGN TRAIL (@ INNSDALE)

The Hollywood Sign Trail is a 5 mile out-and-back that includes The Innsdale Trail, Mulholland Hwy and Mt. Lee Drive. The 700′ elevation gain is spread along the entire route so this slow and steady incline gets a **difficulty of 4/10**. The views of the sign from below are great but be ready to be disappointed at the view of the back of the sign from the top.

↑ Trail VIDEO ↑   ↑ Trail MAP ↑   ↑ Trail WEB PAGE ↑

The Parking – The intersection of Innsdale and Canyon Lake Drive. You've come in from Barham along Lake Hollywood Drive and that turns into Tahoe Drive which dead ends into Canyon Lake Drive. Turn left and you dead end into this street parking Nirvana.

The Best Thing – The first ½ mile of the Innsdale Trail gives you all the cool Hollywood Sign photo ops you really need for your friends from out of town. Ditch the crowds and get your photos and then you can get back to the clubs and beaches where, well, more crowds I guess.

The Route – Despite the Zero Signage to this trailhead, the signage at the trailhead is significant and proves that I wasn't lying. The beginning ½ mile on Innsdale Trail is amazing. Wide, smooth, and great views. When the trail emerges onto the busy Mullholland Highway turn left and fear not, within a few hundred feet you will turn left past all of the "Do Not Enter" barricades.

It is confusing and intimidating on purpose. The practical reason for all the "Go Away" signs is that there is no parking up this cul-de-sac and the zillions of cars a day trying to get to the Hollywood Sign would create gridlock and fistfights before breakfast every morning. The completely intended collateral damage is that most tourists will think that the road is private (it is not) and will turn around and try to follow their Google maps on their phone through the neighborhood streets only to give up and say, "close enough." Not us, right!

Run on past those barricades (you are still on legendary Mulholland by the way. The driving road turns into Ledgewood at this point) and you will just be running down the street past 4 or 5 houses and then – Boom – a chain across the road. Don't sweat it – over the chain – keep on down the now dirt road. Get some water from The Last Water Fountain on Mulholland and – boom – another chain. Around the chain and this dirt trail swings behind another half dozen houses.

This tiny dirt trail becomes a private driveway (don't worry, still legal) that arrives at an impressive gate where there is a kooky, maze-like pedestrian entrance/exit to your left. Take that and head uphill to your left and you are now on Mt Lee Drive. That's the mountain that the Hollywood Sign is on, Mount Lee. Before you head to the top, take the dirt driveway to your left and in 50 feet you are at the classic Hollywood Sign Photo Op dirt-pad. This is your last view of the sign. Turn around now and no one would know it.

Hollywood Sign / Innsdale Trail - 5 miles
Difficulty - 4/10
Parking - Canyon Lake Drive

Elevation Gain - 940' to 1683'
Porta-Potties
No Water

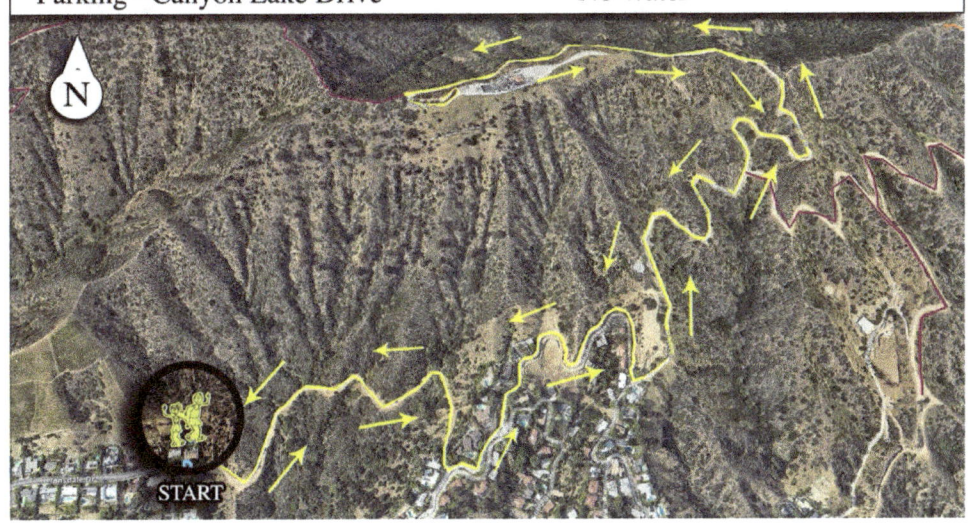

Map data: google earth: image 2024 airbus

Still need to see the top? Okay, back to the asphalt road headed uphill. The only traffic on this road are maintenance vehicles for the fortress of radio antennae at the top and LAPD vehicles chasing down trespassers climbing off-trail to the sign itself. In less than ½ mile you will pass the intersection where the dirt Mulholland Trail enters to the right. Every iteration of Mulholland is sprinkled throughout this area so be ready – Trail, Highway, Drive, Way, Avenue – just be aware.

The entire Mt Lee Drive hike is maybe 1 mile and passes the Mt. Chapel trail at the top and the Wisdom Tree trail at the very tippy top. When you see a cacophony of chain-link fencing, razor wire, and microware transmission towers you know you are almost at one of the most awe-inspiring tourist destinations in the world. The Hollywood Sign. It's almost as disappointing as when you go to Hollywood Blvd and have to run away from a urine-soaked SpongeBob character hitting you up for a dollar.

But you did it. Hike the last uphill dirt section and look at the back of the Hollywood Sign through the fencing and if the smog isn't terrible, you can see Hollywood and beyond. Now head back the way you came. 5 Miles. Boom.

What's the deal with the Hollywood Sign? It was built as Hollywoodland to advertise a new housing neighborhood in 1923. There are entire books about this sign but my favorite facts are: Originally the sign had giant light bulbs all around it flashing "HOLLY" "WOOD" and then "LAND." In 1932 actress Peg Entwistle climbed to the top of the 'H' and then jumped to her death. A songwriter in the 40's Eden Ahbez lived underneath the first 'L' while he was writing Nat King Cole's hit song "Nature Boy." Also check out Hollywoodsign.org.

10 - LAKE HOLLYWOOD LOOP

The Lake Hollywood Loop trail can be 3 or 6 miles and includes the ubiquitous Hollywood Sign selfie spot on Mulholland Hwy. Mostly flat with the option for a slight 200' elevation gain on a dirt trail climb puts the **difficulty at 3/10 or 7/10**. A classic Hollywood Sign view and a truly "locals only" look at Lake Hollywood.

Trail VIDEO   Trail MAP   Trail WEB PAGE

The Parking – Don't just settle for Lake Hollywood Drive right off the bat. Sure, it's the most plentiful and you can see the lake however the coolest spot to park is on Tahoe Drive. If you are coming in from Barham

Blvd (like you should be) drive straight down Lake Hollywood Drive to the lake and continue along the "shoreline" until the road ends and turns left onto Tahoe Drive into the neighborhood. Street park right there.

The Best Thing – Run up the dirt trail to the Hollywood Sign photo-op spot on Mulholland with your tourist friends and the combo of Lake Hollywood, a trail run, and a hassle-free Hollywood Sign photo might make them say, "you know, Los Angeles is not as horrible as people say."

The Route – From your Tahoe Drive parking head down to Lake Hollywood Drive and turn left past the decorative pipe gate blocking the road and then through the gap in the chain link fence blocking the road. The first half of this route is super simple – run for 3 miles clockwise around the lake until you are back here again. Mark. Set. Go!

Okay, maybe some extra information might be helpful. Once you've completed about 2 ½ miles of the loop the road will reconnect with Lake Hollywood drive. The cars driving on that will make it difficult to run on so cross the street and run along the dirt sidewalk for ½ mile until you reach Tahoe Drive and you re-enter the car-free zone.

As you begin your second loop around Lake Hollywood you will notice the lack of shade. Get used to it. That is the only real downside of this trail. However, just before you reach the dam again look up and to the left and you will see another gated chain-link fence designating a new dirt trail heading uphill into the Hollywood Hills. Sure it's a little dusty but that also mikes it slightly less toasty than all that black asphalt you've been on for 4 miles.

It's about 1 mile on a moderate uphill slope with the occasional moderately decent view of the lake however, you will ultimately emerge into the middle of downtown Hollywood Sign tourist photo-palooza. This is Mulholland Drive or Way or Highway… either way, it is were English is truly a second language. Tourists from everywhere and since you didn't park here, it somehow feels less terrible than it might.

Lake Hollywood Loop Trail - 3 or 6 miles
Difficulty - 7/10
Parking - Mineral Wells

Elevation Gain - 788' to 788'
No Restrooms
Unreliable Water Fountain

Map data: google earth: image 2024 airbus

Turn left, downhill, past the dog park, and the first road to your left will be Tahoe Drive. Turn left and run along the suburban sidewalks back down to your car. 6 Miles. Boom.

What's the deal with fence all around Lake Hollywood? In 1923 when LA was building the Hollywood Sign and a bunch of CCC related projects in Griffith Park, Captain Mulholland built the Mulholland Dam which holds back the waters of the mighty Hollywood Reservoir. And because it is a real reservoir that holds drinking water for people below it (They still treat the water with chlorine and some other chemicals before it goes to people's houses. Just not a full water treatment plant or anything) there is a fence all the way around the reservoir to keep all you filthy humans and your poopy dogs from contaminating the water. Some of the water naturally comes from the surrounding hills as rain runoff and ground water. And somehow, I'm still trying to figure this out, the aqueduct system that brings water to LA from the Owens Valley off highway 395 on the way up to Mammoth feeds the Hollywood Reservoir – or Lake Hollywood as we cool people call it.

11 - SKYLINE TRAIL

The Skyline Trail is <u>4.5 miles</u> and includes The Migdal Trail and the Main Horse Trail along interstate 134. The elevation gain of 475′ is spread out and the entire trail is fire road wide making the **difficulty a 3/10.** Views of Forest Lawn and Burbank and IKEA. Not exactly a visitors dream.

Trail VIDEO   Trail MAP   Trail WEB PAGE

The Parking – Let's say you are coming from the Forest Lawn exit off of the 134 (because that's where you should come from) you will be on Zoo Drive and will dead end into Griffith Park Drive at Travel Town. Straight ahead is a hundred civilized paved spots for train tourist but you're not a damned tourist are you? Turn right then quickly left into a dirt, triangular lot that might have 20 parking spots. You're hitting a trail. Get some dirt on your tires.

The Best Thing – The weird picnic area overlooking the Forest Lawn Cemetery at the end of the Migdal Trail. It feels like someone set this up as a destination with palm trees and railings to tie off your horses and tables and… it's just an odd spot at the end of an odd trail.

The Route – Head up the main fire road/horse trail until you reach the ridgetop. Turn right on the ridge and that trail heads down, and then up, and ends at the aforementioned Forest Lawn overlook. It's fine. But look at all the dead people and then turn around.

When you pass the trail you came up on, continue along the ridgeline. You will pass the Rattlesnake Trail that drops down to your right and then comes up on your left. Continue along the ridge pass the old 'illegal' trail to your left that 'used to' go down to Zoo Drive and a cool picnic area. But although it still does… don't go there. Continue along the ridge.

There is a spur that heads off to the right so take it. It dead ends but take it. On a clear day your can see IKEA. It's not worth a selfie or anything but it's not nothing. Okay back to the Skyline ridge trail and you will hit a 'T' where the Condor Trail heads off to the right and the Skyline Trail continues to the left. So go left young man – or woman – or person – whomever you want to be.

The trail passes by the top of the LA zoo so there are fences and signs but it's not like you can peek in and see giraffe heads or anything. As the trail heads back down you will arrive at the ass-end of the LA Zoo parking area. The 'trail' becomes a kind of dirt connector that skirts the parking lot and goes under Zoo Drive through a pretty cool tunnel. You escape the tunnel trolls and hit the main Griffith Park horse trail that parallels the freeway. Turn left.

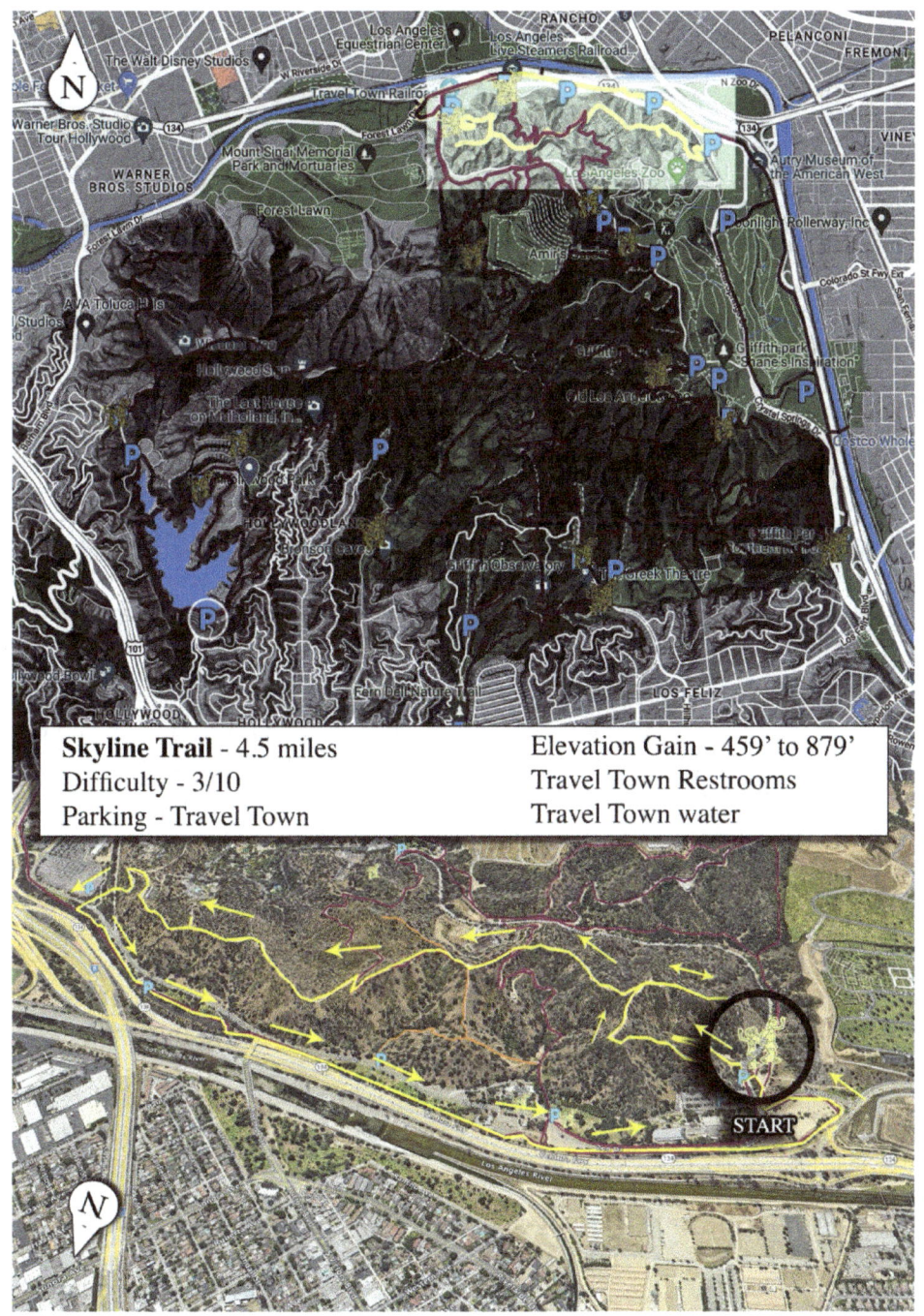

Skyline Trail - 4.5 miles
Difficulty - 3/10
Parking - Travel Town

Elevation Gain - 459' to 879'
Travel Town Restrooms
Travel Town water

Map data: google earth: image 2024 airbus

You now spend almost 2 miles on the horse trail along the freeway. It's loud and you're breathing in exhaust fumes. It's not great but it is flat. So... silver lining? You will pass 2 horse tunnels under I-5 and this is where all those equestrians in Burbank are able to get in to Griffith Park. But you run along and the horse trail ultimately ends but making a U-turn to the left, and then under Forest Lawn Drive, and you end up across the street from where you parked your car. Look both ways, wipe the horse shit off your shoes, and get back into your car. 4.5 Miles. Boom.

What's the deal with the Zoo? In 1966 they closed the old zoo and opened the new zoo. If you've seen the remnants of the old zoo it is obviously a huge upgrade. Some fun facts about the zoo – in the early 2000's there were 35 animal escapes! No kidding! Kangaroos, antelopes, chimpanzees... I mean most are quickly recaptured and returned but did you know that in 1979 a wolf escaped, hid in Griffith Park for a month and it's not really clear if she was ever really caught. Keep your eye out for a 50 year old wolf! Gorillas kept escaping until they build a special Gorilla Reserve in 2007. In 2014 a bighorn sheep escaped and was killed by a car somewhere in Griffith Park. And famously in 2016 the Griffith Park cougar P-22 broke into the zoo and ate a koala named Killarney. Was P-22 annoyed that the koala got a name and she just got a number? I'm sure that was part of it.

12 - TOYON / MINERAL WELLS TRAIL

The Toyon/ Mineral Wells Trail is a 5.5 mile loop and includes Mt. Hollywood Drive, Amir's Garden, The North Trail, Cathy's Corner, and The Haunted Picnic Table! The 800′ elevation gain is spread out and all trails are wide and well used. The views are from Warner Brothers Studios all the way to Burbank. **Difficulty? Let's call it a 6/10.**

Trail VIDEO   Trail MAP   Trail WEB PAGE

The Parking – The 12 dirt spots at the very end of the Mineral Well Picnic Area are my favorites but any of the 100 street parking spots along Mineral Wells is fine.

The Best Thing – The Haunted Picnic Table is along this route and I love a good ghost story, especially one that feels like complete bullshit.

The Route – From the dirt lot there is a trail that heads toward Toyon Canyon. Start there, run towards the skater punks, and then turn right uphill on the dirt trail. This will take you back towards Griffith Park Drive and you will run parallel to that, past the composting area, and to an uphill intersection. Uphill to the left is Toyon Trail but we are continuing forward and down hill.

At the bottom of the incline is a gated off road to your left. This is Mt. Hollywood Drive and the Mecca of all Griffith Park cyclists. Turn left because you are joining the cyclists today. You are going to run up on this Asphalt road for 2 miles and it's actually mostly shaded and nice. Just before you reach the top, the Hauted Picnic Table is on your right. It's not much to look at but the story is pretty great.

At the top there is a rare asphalt road – asphalt road intersection. Turn left, downhill, and you are now on Vista Del Valle Drive. Not for long because the next trail on your left is the North Trail and you will take that. The North Trail drops down to run along Toyo Canyon. In the middle of the canyon there is a significant right turn past a large Water Tank. Turn Right here.

You will now run straight into Amir's Garden but before you do, turn left and the trail will take you back to the Mineral Well Picnic Area. However, you've parked on the far side so take the trail to your left and that is a fantastic flat and shady ¼ mile cool down. 5.5 miles. Boom.

What's the deal with the Haunted Picnic Table? In 1976 on Halloween night (let's face it, a ghost story that purportedly happened on Halloween night is already only 50% believable) two young lovers Rand and Nancy were doing their young lover business on this picnic table when the branch of this tree broke off and killed them both! When a park employee went to remove the tree he heard voices saying, "Leave. Us. Alone." So he did. But his co-worker called him a wussie and on a $500 bet went up to remove the tree himself. Later that day, that guy… found dead on the site. Since then, no one will remove that tree. It is there today and 45 years after the fall, the tree has never rotted! Dun. Dun. Duuuuuun!

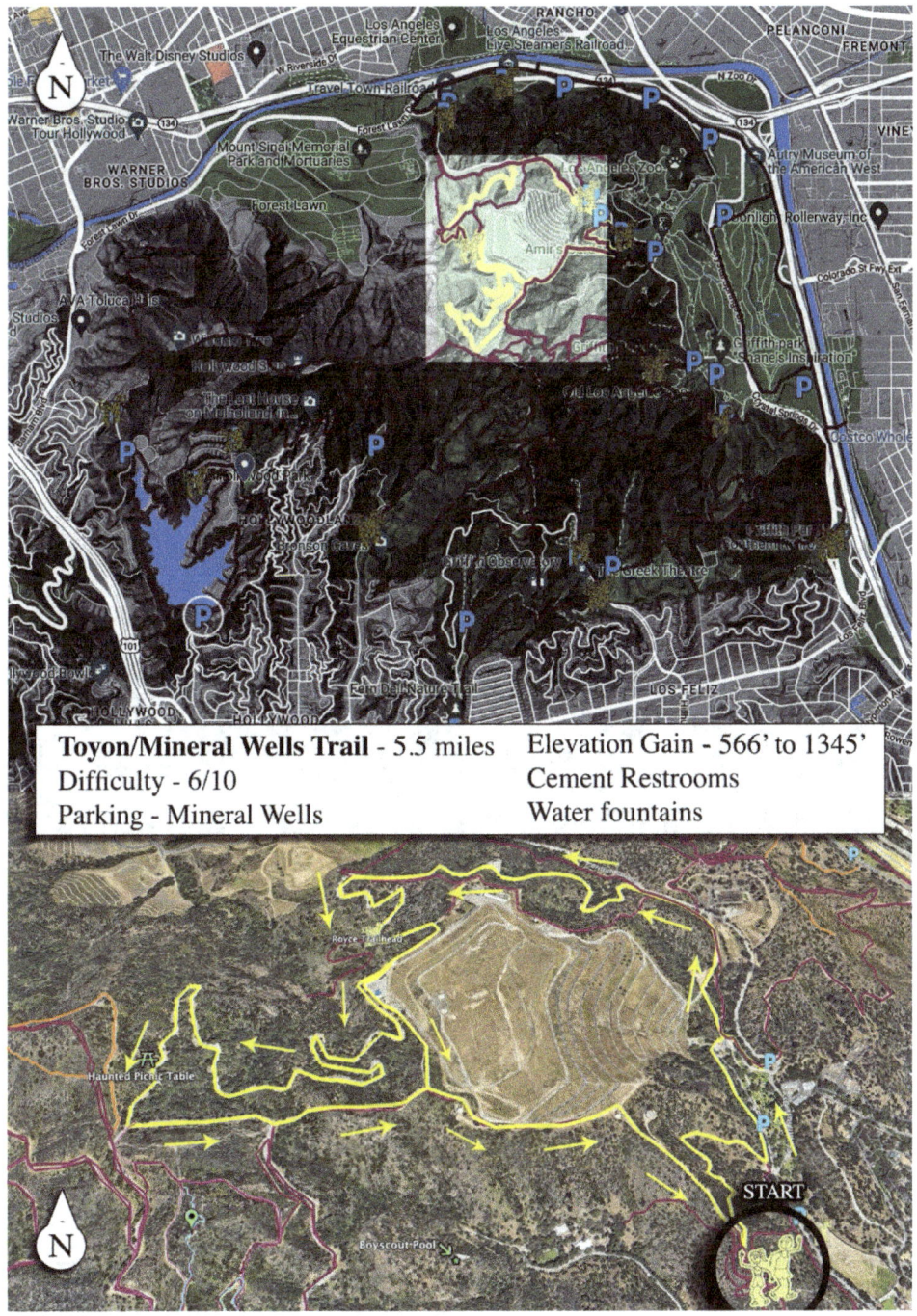

Toyon/Mineral Wells Trail - 5.5 miles
Difficulty - 6/10
Parking - Mineral Wells
Elevation Gain - 566' to 1345'
Cement Restrooms
Water fountains

Map data: google earth: image 2024 airbus

Toyon Canyon

It's not much of a canyon anymore because from 1957 to 1985 the city of Los Angeles filled the canyon with garbage. It'd be nice to think that they reached a moment of enlightenment in the 70's and said, "Hey man, this isn't cool for the environment man. We gotta find a smarter alternative that is better for Los Angeles and all humans who live here!" and then worked tirelessly to find alternatives. Nope. They only stopped when it was declared full in 1985.

So LA covered it up and was going to convert it back to a recreation area with trees planted and big bushes and such. However someone realized that the roots of larger bushes and trees would pierce the protective shell or coating or whatever is keeping down the escaping methane so now it's just a weird, stepped field forever. And that methane? It is channeled into an electric power station at the top of the hill that burns that methane and powers 4,500 homes a years. Houses powered by garbage! I think we all know which homes in our neighborhood are running on garbage power.

Royce's Canyon

Royce Neuschatz was a Parks Commissioner from 1978 to 1984. During that time she (That's right you rotten sexist, Royce is a lady name! And… I didn't know that until I just now read her obituary online. Spoiler alert. She's dead) anyway, when Toyon Canyon filled up to the top with garbage, jerks at the city were thinking, "Well, let's just start filling up the next canyon over." But Royce wasn't having any of it. She fought 'em. She was a fighter. Environmentalist. Preservationist. Activist. Back in those days they just called her a "tree hugger" and she saved this canyon.

So look for this sign as you are riding up Mount Hollywood Drive. Maybe you're not on a bike but a lot of bikes come up this way. It's the piped off asphalt road just above the compost area. Go hike down this ¼ mile trail one day, there are a couple of groovy caves and an intermittent creek!

13 - WISDOM TREE TRAIL

The Wisdom Tree Trail is a 3 mile out-and-back that includes a trek past Cahuenga Peak over to The Hollywood Sign. The 800′ gain is the first 3/4 mile and it is steep, hot, and crowded while the scramble to the Hollywood Sign requires actual climbing giving this a **difficulty rating of 8/10**. Views of Lake Hollywood and Warner Brothers Studios are phenomenal.

⬆ Trail VIDEO ⬆   ⬆ Trail MAP ⬆   ⬆ Trail WEB PAGE ⬆

The Parking – Lake Hollywood road from the Lake Hollywood reservoir straight uphill to Wonderview Drive has 8 zillion parking spots so try and park as close to the top as possible. On the weekend it fills up, especially later in the day. But don't quit on it! You will find something.

The Best Thing – At the base of the Wisdom Tree is usually – less often recently – a metal ammo box with journals and pens where you can write a poem or read other people's poems. Who is in charge of this? That's a good question.

The Route – From your parked car hike up to the top and turn right onto the neighborhood street Wonderview Drive. Eight houses later you will arrive at a Jurassic Park sized fence and gate. It's open all day and locked all night. Don't be intimidated but don't hang out and watch the sunset!

After you pass through the gate the road will turn from asphalt to dirt and in 50 yards there will be access to a reservoir to the left. Don't bother, keep heading forward and you will see an old fence to the left that blocks the road used by the high power electric line people. Don't bother, keep heading forward and you will see a plaque from The Trust for Public Land donating Cahuenga Peak. The trail begins just to the left of the plaque.

FYI, Cahuenga Peak is a mound between the Wisdom Tree and The Hollywood Sign that we will walk over but honestly, it' kinda meh. Sorry Trust for Public Land.

Back to the trail. You now head up a busy, well worn, rocky single track hiking trail. It may only be ¾ of a mile up to the ridge, but there is no shade and the elevation gain is significant. And did I mention? It's busy.

At the top of the ridge you will see the tree to your left. So walk over there and look at the flags and cairns and journals and people… there is usually a lot going on. The view of Warner Brothers studios and Burbank are pretty great as is the view of Lake Hollywood and downtown Hollywood. Okay, enough of that. Turn around and head back along the trail along the ridge.

Pass the trail you came up on and head towards The Hollywood Sign. Before the halfway point of Cahuenga Peak you will pass a scrubby, rain-washed trail to your left. Remember that for later. When you arrive at Cahuenga peak there will be a clearing with a metal geographical disk marking the official summit hammered into the ground. Like I said before, Meh.

The remaining ¼ mile is downhill and has some significant drops requiring hand holds and root grabbing. You will need to have two hands to finish this part of the hike! Finally, you will emerge onto Mount Lee Drive where you are 200 yards from the top of The Hollywood Sign.

Turn right along this asphalt road and you will see the back of the Hollywood Sign to your right behind a long run of chain link fence. It's not great. Pass that is a utility yard filled with antennae. Also not great. Loop up before that to your left and you are at the Hollywood Sign overlook. Again, not great. But technically, you have hiked up to the Hollywood Sign.

Now head back where you came from and if you just head straight back down to your car, this is a 3.5 mile trail. However, remember that scrubby, rain-washed trail I mention near Cahuenga Peak, you can take that to your right and you are in for an additional 1.5 miles of adventure!

This overgrown trail heads down for 1 mile towards Forest Lawn Drive and finally intersects with the Power Line access road. Turn left on that and you have about ½ along this uphill route that is surprisingly interesting and remote. Ultimately you will arrive at the intersection you were at earlier just before the Trust for Public Lands plaque. From here, downhill to your car. 5 Miles. Boom.

Wisdom Tree Trail - 3 miles
Difficulty - 8/10
Parking - Lake Hollywood Road

Elevation Gain - 952' to 1814'
No Restrooms
No Water

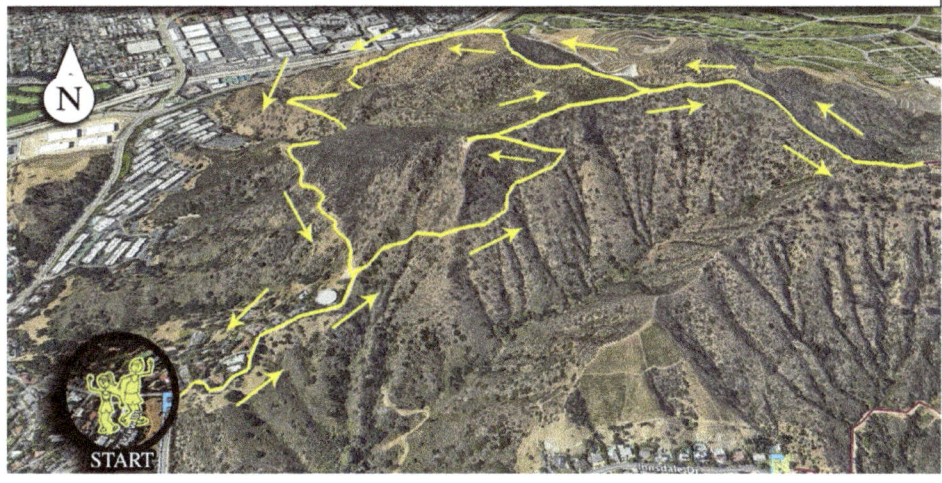

Map data: google earth: image 2024 airbus

What's the deal with this tree? People call it lots of things: Wisdom Tree, Tree of Life, Wishing Tree, Tree of Wonder, Steve. Rumor has it that 35 years ago McDonalds was giving away free trees. That's a real thing! You'd get a "McWish" tree with your happy meal. So somebody planted their McWish tree up here. Other rumors say that a weird group led by a guy with the weird name of Smirch one year brought their live Christmas trees up here, planted them, and one of them actually took. However it got here, it was the only thing that survived the 2007 Barham fire. If you know your history/fairy tales, you'll know that this could have only happened with the magical protection of Wood Nymphs.

14 - RATTLESNAKE / CONDOR / OAK TRAIL

The Rattlesnake/ Condor/ Oak Trail is a 4 mile loop that includes The Skyline Trail. The 525' elevation gain is mostly at the beginning and puts the **difficulty level at a modest 5/10**. Views of Burbank and IKEA are what they should be… mediocre.

Trail VIDEO   Trail MAP   Trail WEB PAGE

The Parking – There are about 30 dirt spots at the Rattlesnake trailhead. It can have water filled pot holes long after any rain storm just FYI. This is also the parking area for the Live Steamers Train Museum. This is the "small train" parking not the "big train" parking. And don't worry, there is also plenty of street parking along Zoo Drive and another giant dirt lot across the street.

The Best Thing – Well, if you didn't know about the free compost area in Griffith Park you get to see where that is. I mean, it's a nice short run but nothing really to tell your friends about.

The Route – From the enormous trailhead sign and map begin uphill with a decent elevation gain and past the 2 water tanks on your left. When you reach the ridgetop turn left and you are now on the Skyline Trail. There will be a spur trail to an overlook to your right. Take it or don't. We didn't today but have in the past.

Continuing on the Skyline Trail there will be a slight downhill and you will reach a large intersection. Turn right here. This is the beginning of the Condor Trail. This chunk lasts about ½ mile and spits you out at the end of the Mineral Wells picnic area. Cross Griffith Park Drive and keep to your right through the dirt parking lot and the trail will head towards the bottom of Toyon (the old city dump) Canyon. Turn right, uphill, before you get to Toyon and the trail will bring you back along Griffith Park Drive.

Here's where you might see cars filling up with free compost. Make a mental note and continue on the trail uphill parallel to the road. The trail peaks and there is a route that peels off to the left (Toyon Trail). Don't take that, continue forward and downhill. You are now on The Oak Canyon Trail.

This parallels the road until the bottom where, if you were a horse, you could continue forward underneath Forest Lawn Drive. Instead, turn right and cross the street as if you were headed to Travel Town. Run past Travel Town in the bike lane along Zoo Drive because you are parked in the dirt lot on the other side of Travel Town. Remember? 4 miles. Boom.

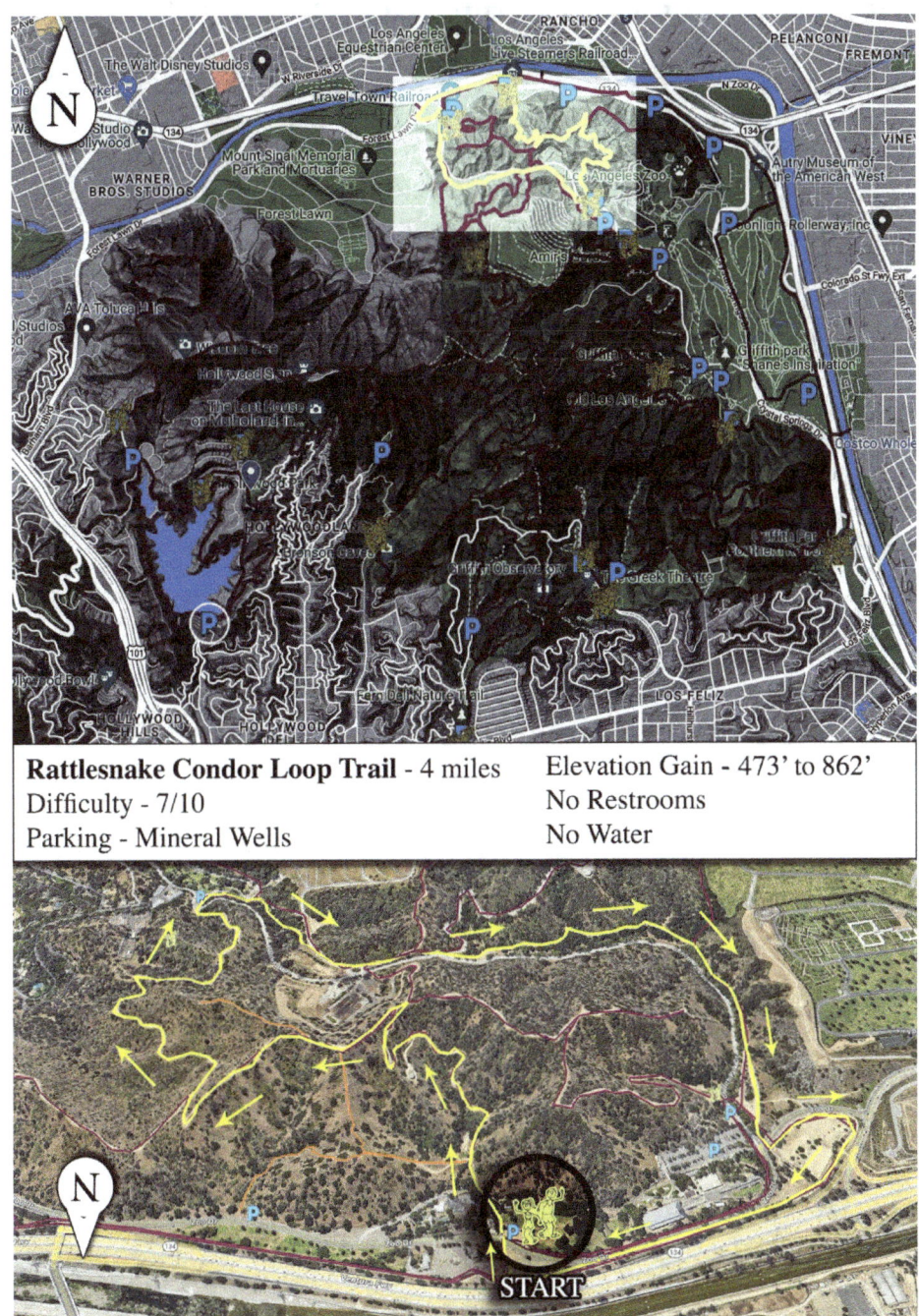

Rattlesnake Condor Loop Trail - 4 miles
Difficulty - 7/10
Parking - Mineral Wells

Elevation Gain - 473' to 862'
No Restrooms
No Water

Map data: google earth: image 2024 airbus

What's the deal with the free compost deal? Well, it's free! Griffith Park takes green clippings from the park, mixes it with the horse poop it picks up off the trails every day. And the Zoo Poo – only from vegetarian animals. Think about it, that makes sense, right? Then they add "bio-solids" from a city wastewater treatment plant. Mix that all up and let it sit and TaDa. Mulchy Compost! They definitely have different batches on different days. When you pull up sometimes it's more mulchy and sometimes it's more compostey. Sometimes there's not much and sometimes there is, literally, a shit-ton. But it's free so beggars can't be complainers, right? Bring your own shovel and some buckets to fill up.

Train Town

Used to be a prisoner of war camp during WW2 for Italians, Germans, and Japanese. That's a long commute to house prisoners but I think they were mostly Americans that the FBI thought were suspicious collaborators with the enemy so, when in doubt… throw 'em in a prison camp. It was also a Japanese internment camp. I don't know why you'd capture Japanese in the Pacific or around the country, then bring them to California, mix them in with American Japanese citizens that you've decided were all spies.

This place opened for prison camping in 1941 and in 1943 turned into an Army photography center… of course. Griffith Park tried to cover up all that nastiness and just talk about trains whenever people would come by this area however there were too many Japanese survivors. They got tired of that bullshit and said, "Hey, that's bullshit," and in 2023 (that's not one of my poorly researched stats, that's real - 2023) they finally put up a plaque admitting to their (our) bullshit.

15 - RATTLESNAKE / SUICIDE TRAIL

The Rattlesnake/ Suicide Trail is a 3 mile loop that includes the Oak Canyon Trail and the Toyon Trail. The moderate elevation gain combined with a steep and skinny Suicide Trail puts the **difficulty at 6/10.** A view of Forest Lawn is all you get.

↑ Trail VIDEO ↑   ↑ Trail MAP ↑   ↑ Trail WEB PAGE ↑

The Parking – There are about 30 dirt spots at the Rattlesnake trailhead. It can have water filled pot holes long after any rain storm just FYI. This is also the parking area for the Train Museum. This is the "small train" parking not the "big train" parking. And don't worry, there is also plenty of street parking along Zoo Drive and another giant dirt lot across the street

The Best Thing – The steep and skinny Suicide Trail is a welcome change of pace from the mainly wide and dusty horse trails of Griffith Park. Some may disagree (Freya) but I also like that. It eliminates the fraidy cats and momma's boys for just a little while.

The Route – From the enormous trailhead sign and map begin uphill with a decent elevation gain and past the 2 water tanks on your left. When you reach the ridge a quick right turn then left turn back down hill keeps you on the Rattlesnake Trail. You will pass the Griffith Park Composting area on your left and then cross Griffith Park Drive. It's a real road with real cars so pay attention.

On the other side of the road you will turn right uphill on a large fire road. Quickly, at the next intersection you will veer left, uphill, while the main trail continues forward and downhill. You are now on the Toyon Trail and after some more elevation gain as you will see Toyon Canyon to your left. As you are almost past Toyon (the former city dump) Canyon there will be an intersection. Right is more Toyon Trail and straight ahead is Mulholland Drive.

Right turn is a short and sweet little connecting trail over to Mulholland Drive however… if you can't get enough of chain link fence and crumbling asphalt and methane gas processing buildings, you can continue forward and scramble around some confusing dead ends and detours and you will still arrive at Mulholland Drive, just much further up the road. If you decide to do this, when you hit Mulholland Drive, turn right. And don't worry, this is a "no cars" road so worst-case scenario, a cyclist rudely passes too close to you.

After a quarter mile of Mulholland you will meet up with the short Toyon Trail that you had passed up earlier. It's to your right and there is good signage and everything. So from here turn around and look uphill on big old asphalt Mulholland. There at the top where the road turns left, you will go straight ahead into the brush.

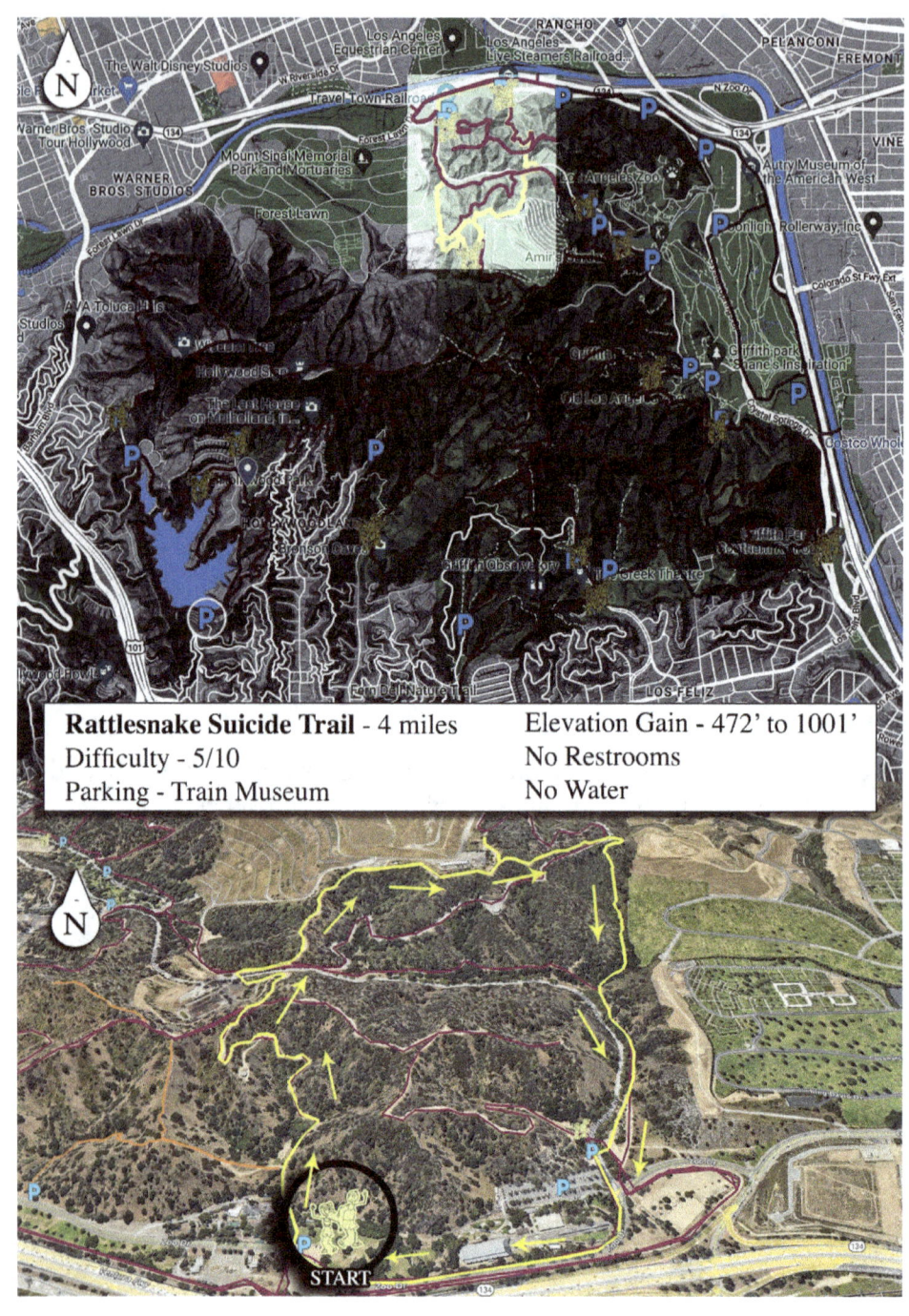

Rattlesnake Suicide Trail - 4 miles
Difficulty - 5/10
Parking - Train Museum

Elevation Gain - 472' to 1001'
No Restrooms
No Water

Map data: google earth: image 2024 airbus

This beginning of the Suicide Trail is not marked but depending upon the time of year it is easier to see or not. Leave the asphalt and head towards the Forest Lawn fence. You will notice the small trail heading downhill paralleling the fence line. Yes, it is overgrown, and yes you have to duck and grab branches that are in your way, and yes, some areas are slick and sandy… That makes it fun, right?

After a couple hundred yards you will emerge onto the classic Griffith Park horse trail Oak Canyon. This parallels Griffith Park Drive and you will take it downhill to where it connects over to Travel Town at Forest Lawn Drive. But since our car is down the road a piece, let's follow the horses and take the tunnel straight ahead of us that goes under Forest Lawn Drive and loops around to loll along the peaceful and majestic 134 freeway. 100 yards of that is enough so cut through the dirt lot to your right when you see your parking area at the "small train" parking lot. 3.75 miles. Boom.

What's the deal with Forest Lawn? The Forest Lawn that we all think of in Griffith Park is actually considered the "Hollywood Hills" Forest Lawn. The second Forest Lawn. The original is in Atwater Village off of San Fernando Blvd and S Glendale Ave. But the Griffith Park Forest Lawn was built in 1950 and is in the style of the original Forest Lawn which invented the "Memorial Park" or the "Lawn Park" whereas until 1906 all cemeteries were just acres of headstones. Go to the east coast. You'll see it right away. So the big, open lawn with no headstones cemeteries that you see in lots of places around the country?... that was invented by the Forest Lawn people!

16 - OLD ZOO LOOP TRAIL

The Old Zoo Loop Trail is a <u>1.4 mile loop</u> that runs along the remains of the Old Zoo which only held 15 animals when it started so yeah, it's small. It used to be easy to climb over a low fence and into each animal cage. A lot of infected gorilla student films were shot here. However, the city has been putting up stronger and stronger fences to keep us humans out. Short and mostly flat, it's stroller and grandma friendly with a **difficulty of 1/10.**

The Parking – You can park anywhere near the carousel in Griffith Park. The first lot above the tennis courts is closest but the second lot near the playground area will have more spots open. Even on a crowded day if you just keep circling something will open up. Have faith!…and some patience.

The Best Thing – The graffiti covered creek (Bee Rock Creek maybe?) is not as sketchy as it sounds and the three animal cages that are kept open for picnicking are not as animal poopy as they sound.

The Route – Get over to where your car first entered the parking lot. The pipe gate that stops cars let's people through. A dozen yards uphill from there is the sign for the Fern Canyon Trailhead. Continue uphill and take the first right turn. It will have a sign that says "Old Zoo Trail."

Now you are on mostly flat trail above the carousel and soon you will begin seeing old zoo cages. Old zoo cement boxes with bars and cages in the back. Most have been fenced up by the city, but people keep "reestablishing access." If you're curious, tug on a fence. You might get in.

After about ½ mile you'll see Trump's metal border fence on the right that will keep you out of the coolest old zoo cages. If you continue around the fence to the right you will see the three legal cages set up as picnic areas. It's fine, but let's continue the loop uphill a little bit.

Another hundred yards and you will reach the mighty Bee Rock Creek. Cross it and follow it uphill to the upper old zoo trail. Turn left and you will be returning towards your car just uphill a bit. Surprisingly, it's just enough to give you a pretty amazing view of the mountains beyond Glendale… smog permitting.

You will quickly dead end into the Fern Valley Trail where a left turn downhill will take you back to the parking lot. 1.4 miles. Boom.

Old Zoo Loop Trail - 1.4 miles
Difficulty - 2/10
Parking - Carousel

Elevation Gain - 518' to 709'
Cement Restrooms
Water Fountains

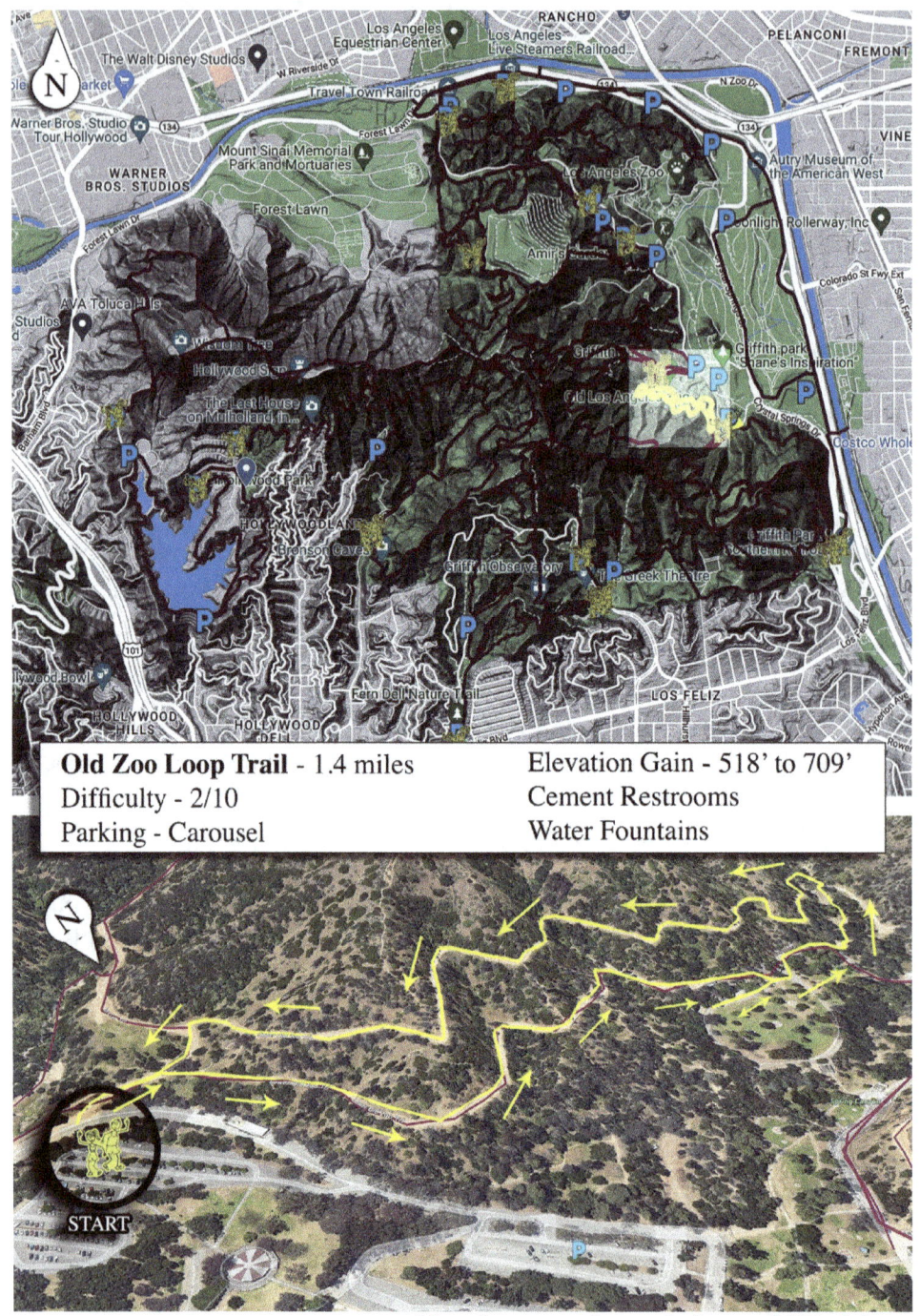

Map data: google earth: image 2024 airbus

What's the deal with the old zoo? Built in 1912 on the location of Griffith J. Griffith's old ostrich farm the old zoo started with 15 animals, most of which were from private movie makers who had exotic animals for their movies. Soon the animal population grew to 100 animals including bobcats, deer, monkeys and deer. Apparently this janky zoo was always on the brink of closing. They had a famous camel named Bactrian who had both humps disfigured in a Ringling Brothers Circus train accident. Tortoises would fight with other animals. Zebras and bears broke their necks. Big cats died from eating tainted horse meat. It was a hot mess that just kept rolling along somehow. In 1958 citizens voted to pay for a "real" zoo and in 1966 the old zoo shut down and we got the real zoo that we have today.

17 – GREEK / HOGBACK TRAIL LOOP

The Greek Theater Hogback Trail Loop is about 4 miles. It tops out at Mt. Hollywood and the uphill to that is "indirect." We head up the Riverside Trail (dumb, because it's not near a river ever) and hit the Hogback Trail which is a challenging uphill for about a mile.(didn't see a single hog) 360 views at the top of the Tom LaBonge Overlook and 1.5 miles back down. **A solid 8/10 of Griffith Park difficulty**.

↱ Trail VIDEO ↰   ↱ Trail MAP ↰   ↱ Trail WEB PAGE ↰

The Paring – The parking lot above the Greek Theater is your first stop unless... the Greek Theater is using it. If it is, do a different trail today. On a nice day, the lot fills quickly so as you are driving up Vermont Ave from Los Feliz keep your head on a swivel and snatch any parking spot that's open once you're in sight of The Greek!

The Best Thing – The 1 mile uphill scramble on the Hogback Trail is the reason to take this route. There are easier routes to the top of Mt. Hollywood. But you come to this trail for the burn. The butt burn. The Gluteus Maximus workout-i-mus.

The Route – Imagine that you've parked above the Greek Theater. Now cross the street and a pretty prominent trailhead sign says – Riverside Trailhead. Start running.

The first mile is mellow and mostly above the tennis courts. Oh yeah, there are 12 public pay-to-play courts above Riverside Drive. You can barely hear them or see them. Just keep running.

The end of the mile starts to get a little steep and when you reach the intersection with Vista Del Valle Road, you will do a 270 degree left turn at the green shed and head back up on the Hogback Trail.

The next mile is a significant scramble. Uphill. Slippery rocks covered in sand. Lots of people resting and taking a knee. It's great, but a challenging kind of great.

Towards the top you pass Dante's Peak which is a garden filled with… garden stuff. But we're still running, right? Continue on and there is a sharp left turn that takes you up to the highest point in Griffith Park, Mt. Hollywood.

Great views. Spin around. And back down. Keep your eyes open to the left as there is a tricky trail that heads you down towards the Griffith Observatory. We are not going there, just going TOWARDS there. Watch the video. This kind of trail is why I make these videos. Please. Stop reading, and find the video.

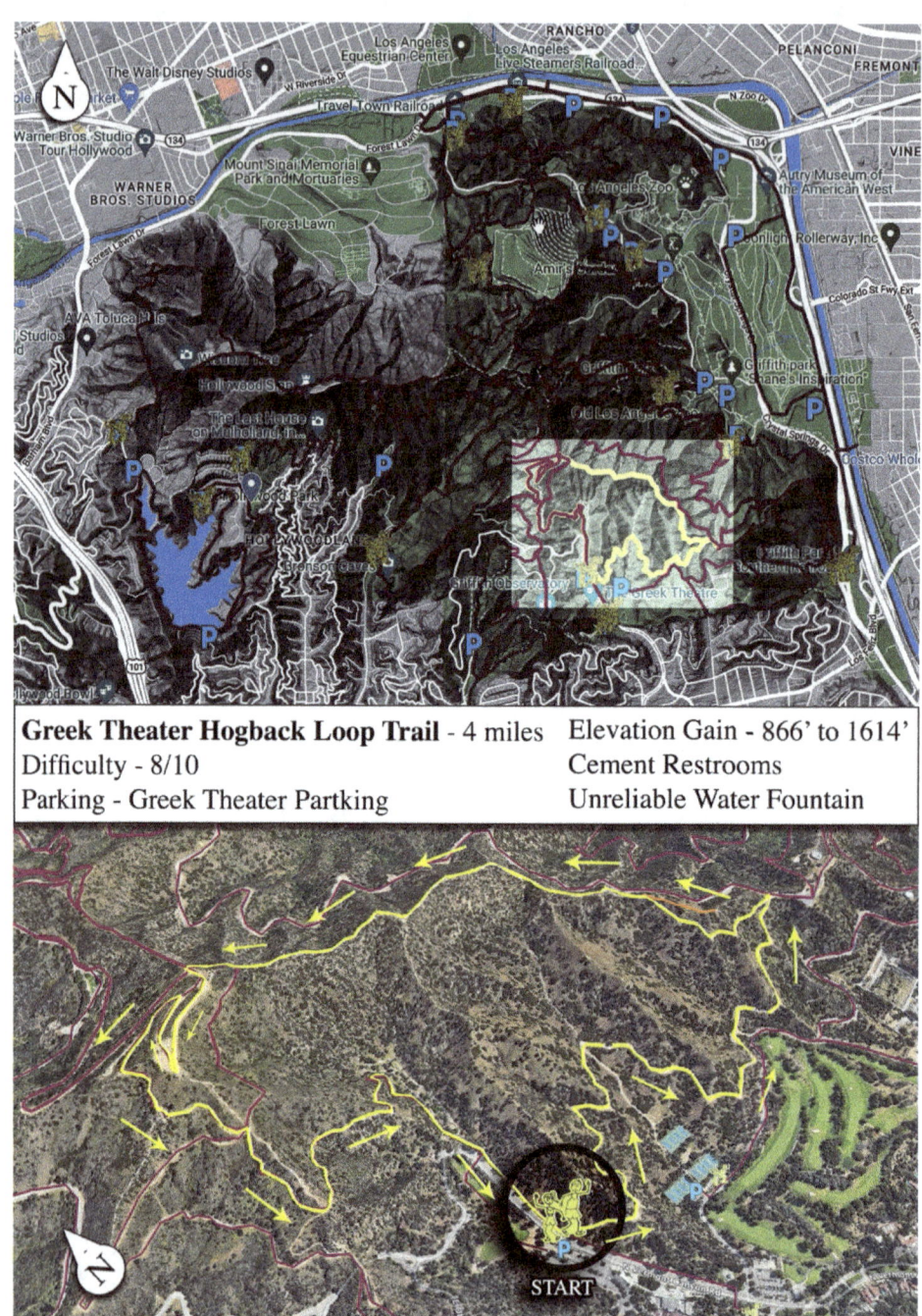

Greek Theater Hogback Loop Trail - 4 miles
Difficulty - 8/10
Parking - Greek Theater Partking

Elevation Gain - 866' to 1614'
Cement Restrooms
Unreliable Water Fountain

Map data: google earth: image 2024 airbus

So now you are heading downhill and whenever you see the Griffith Observatory you are turning away from it to your left and low and behold, you end up past the sometimes, and always sketchy, bird sanctuary, and back to your car. 4 Miles. Boom.

Griffith Observatory

It's free! I mean the planetarium show costs $10 which you should do if you are touristing. But if you live in town and just curious there are cool solar, sun flare, astronomy exhibits up there that are great for kids and great for curious older humans. I know the $10/hour parking up there is a kick in the sack but if you have anyone in your group that has the slightest difficulty, you gotta do that.

There is a great view of the Hollywood Sign from up here and if you park up here, you might as well hike up to Mount Hollywood. It's some work, but if it's a clear day?... LA will look like the gem it is portrayed as in old Hollywood movies or on Hollywood Blvd postcards.

What's the deal with Mt Hollywood?

This view is the deal!

18 - COMMONWEALTH LOOP TRAIL

The Commonwealth Loop Trail is about 4 miles. Starting at the tennis courts above the Roosevelt golf course this route heads over towards Beacon Hill and then back along the fancy Los Feliz neighborhoods. The first half of the trail is a steady uphill on pavement while the return trip has some very steep dirt sections with a crazy elevation gain of 1100' in ¼ mile to get up to Cedar Grove. Going for a workout? This trail **is 9/10 difficulty.** Don't want a workout? Turn around at Cedar Grove and this is 2 out of 10.

↑ Trail VIDEO ↑   ↑ Trail MAP ↑   ↑ Trail WEB PAGE ↑

The Parking – The left side of the parking lot at the tennis courts is for us. Non-tennis players. If that's full, there is street parking along the golf course.

If that's full, you are stuck parking on Vermont with the rabble near the Greek Theater.

The Best Thing – Cedar Grove is a cool spot. Figuratively and literally. If you want to sit, peace out, and meditate, I'd say this is the best spot in Griffith Park to do that.

The Route – Let us begin at the tennis courts. Start along Commonwealth Road at the pipe gate where your car isn't allowed. Along the golf course you will pass a couple of tee boxes so remember not to be obnoxiously loud. Even though you're not golfing, it's polite to observe some golf etiquette.

Within a quarter mile you turn left, uphill, past another yellow pipe gate onto Vista Del Valle Road. After .5 miles on your right, you will see Cedar Grove. There's a nice sign to remind you where you came from and where you are going. Well right now you should pop in to the Cedar Grove, It's a hundred yards in, nice and chill and then come back the Vista Del Valle.

The back side of Cedar grove does connect to a trail that returns back to Commonwealth Drive, but we are going to pretend we don't know that just to add a couple miles to this route.

Continuing up the Asphalt Vista Del Valle we will arrive at our peak, the Joey Klass water station. Turn right here and head down the dirt trail towards Beacon Hill. A hundred yards and we'll hit the 5 point intersection where we will take another hard right heading towards the old pony rides.

There is a small trail to your right after about 1 mile down hill. See the sign that points you to Council Road? And head that direction but quickly you will take the first side trail into the brush to your right.

Here is where we leave civilization and signs and laws. From here we will head uphill for half a mile. There are a couple side trails to your left that go into the neighborhoods but veer right, and uphill. It's like a 30 degree slope. And you top out at… Cedar Grove. When you do, turn around and behold, an amazing view of Atwater Village. It's a combination of the steep slope below your and the neighborhoods to your right that make it more interesting than other Griffith Park views… I dunno. It's just cool.

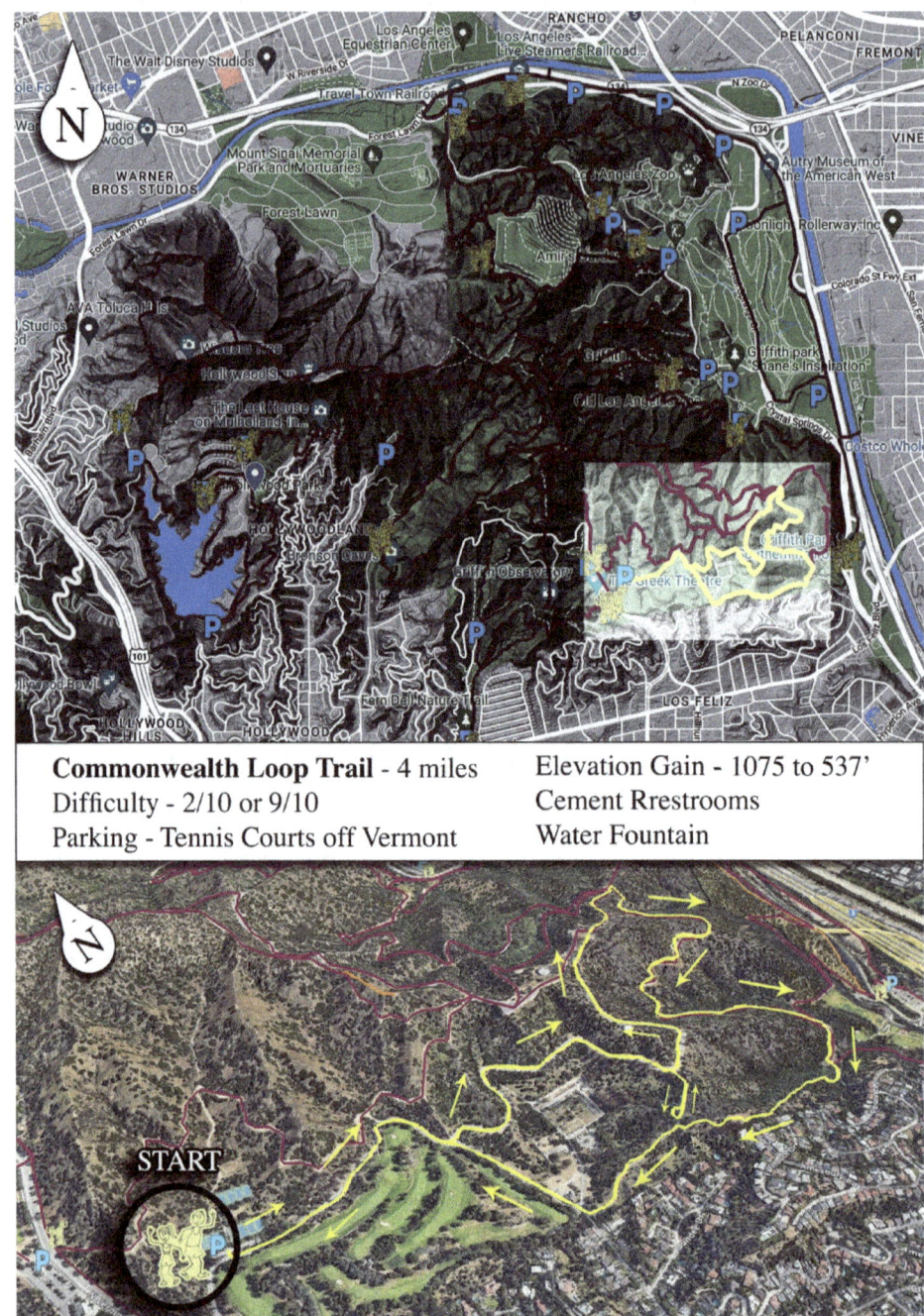

Commonwealth Loop Trail - 4 miles
Difficulty - 2/10 or 9/10
Parking - Tennis Courts off Vermont

Elevation Gain - 1075 to 537'
Cement Rrestrooms
Water Fountain

Map data: google earth: image 2024 airbus

Okay, continue on this small trail past the Cedar Grove and you will start downhill along a quickly steepening trail. It's slick and sandy and you will doubt my directions because it's not a great trail but… it is legit and ends at the other side of Commonwealth Drive.
Here you turn right, past the yellow pipe gate, with the golf course to your left and run back to where you parked, connecting your loop.4 Miles. Boom.

What's the deal with the Cedar Grove? Mysteriously planted maybe in the 1930's with trees left over from the building of Fern Dell maybe? But Cedars aren't native to this area or in Fern Dell but the Civilian Conservation Corps (CCC) and the Works Progress Administration (WPA) did a bunch of stuff in Griffith Park so since there is no record of why this Cedar Grove happened everyone just assumes that some rogue band of CCCers or WPAers rolled over here and just built this. Also, I read that Cedar Grove was used in the movie Die Hard but… John McClane was in Nakatomi Tower the whole time. I call BS on that.

19 - MAIN TRAIL

The Main Trail is a <u>10 mile loop</u> with zero elevation gain along the 134 freeway and Interstate 5. We begin at the Los Feliz entrance where the Pony Rides (RIP ponies) used to be. From that train ride area we run 5 miles over to the Forest Lawn entrance of Griffith Park to the other train ride area, and back again. Freeway noise and horse poop. It's not for most people. However... flat. So there's that. **Difficulty 1/10**

↑ Trail VIDEO ↑   ↑ Trail MAP ↑   ↑ Trail WEB PAGE ↑

The Parking - Remember the pony rides right off of Los Feliz Blvd. off of Crystal Spring Drive? That whole business is closed but you can still do the train ride there and that parking lot is the perfect lot to begin this trail. Decent bathrooms, water fountains. The snack bar serves burgers and stuff on the weekends. Easily 50 paved spots

However, you can park in any parking area along this route and there are a dozen areas. All free. Zoo parking is free. Travel Town parking is free. There are spots all along Zoo Drive where you can just pull to the side.

The Best Thing - The flatness. If you are pushing a stroller or trying out a new hip, this is a rare 10 miles of continuous flat.

The Route - We are running from the ex-pony ride/ Southern Train Ride area to the Travel Town Train Ride area near Forest Lawn and back again. You can flip it. I'm not your mom. But for now just listen up to this plan. Geeze.

Get to the north end of the parking lot. Past the Cafe and the virtual reality ride-pod-thing you will see a large horse trail with the big railings and everything. This starts you along Interstate 5.

The next 2.5 miles will be between the freeway and Crystal Springs Drive. There is a horse tunnel on your right in less than 1 mile that connects to a bridge across the LA river over to Atwater Village. It's interesting. Go check it out once. That should be enough for most people.

Continuing on you will pass the golf course to your left. You will pass behind the Gene Autry Museum but don't look for any signs. They don't put signs between their behind and the freeway.

When you can see the zoo across the street to your left you are no longer between Crystal Springs and The 5, you are now between Zoo Drive and The 134 freeway.

Continue for 2 more miles and you will reach a large horse tunnel to your right that connects with the Burbank Equestrian Center. Pass that and circle around the horse training ring to your left. This will take you under Forest Lawn Drive (Last poopy horse tunnel. I promise.) where you are now across the street from Travel Town.

Main Trail - 10 miles
Difficulty - 1/10
Parking - Old Pony Rides lot

Elevation Gain - - 413' to 538'
Flush toilets, mini-cafe, train rides
Water Fountains

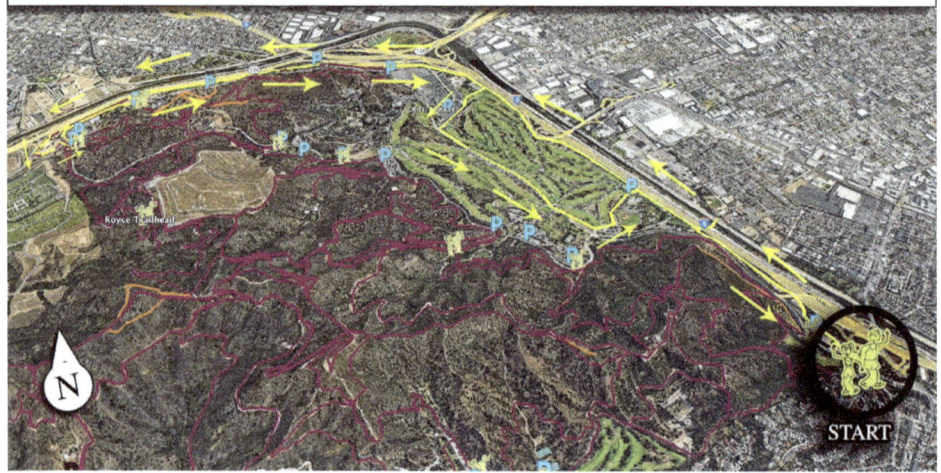

Map data: google earth: image 2024 airbus

Cross the street and for half a mile you are running on asphalt in the bike lane on the road back the way you came. Don't think of it as "road-running", think of it as "racing the choo-choo trains." Funner, right? Now you are returning along the 134 and then the 5 until you reach the golf course. (Now on your right, 'cause you turned around, get it?) Take the horse trail to your right before the golf course and you will now go run along Crystal Springs Drive and the Golf Course.

If you are wearing your sexy running gear, this is a good place to show off to all of the "car drivers" and "afraid to exercisers". Continue to round the golf course on your left and you will hit the Main Trail once again.
Turn right and in little over 1 mile you will arrive at the ex-pony & cafe parking area. 10ish miles. Boom.

What's the deal with The Zoo?

It's a great zoo. It's $22 bucks. Parking is free. If you live in town, buy the $90 dollar year-long (includes one guest) membership.

What about The Autry Museum?

It's a pretty small museum. You walk in and the first thing you see are old clay pots. If you want to spend $18 bucks to look at old clay pots, this is the place for you. I'll meet you afterwards at a food truck out front.

95

20 - BIKE ROUTE

This Griffith Park Bike route is <u>19 miles</u>. Starting at the bike rental shipping container between the Ranger Station/ Visitor's Center and the softball field this route passes The LA Zoo, Travel Town, The Observatory, The Greek Theater, Bee Rock, and all golf courses. The 800' elevation gain over 3 miles above Travel Town puts the **difficulty up to 7 out of 10.**

↑ Trail VIDEO ↑   ↑ Trail MAP ↑   ↑ Trail WEB PAGE ↑

The Parking – When you're driving in on Crystal Springs Road from Los Feliz, turn right just before you get to the Carousel parking. This leads to the Crystal Spring Picnic Area but you start looking for parking right away. If you are bringing your own bike, hell you can start anywhere you like, but

I'm starting us all at the bike rental container. Because I'm a blue-collar man of the people… and I don't own a bike.

The Best Thing – Riding on Mt. Hollywood Drive before you get to The Griffith Observatory there is a bench right where the trail from Bronson Caves comes in. The view of the observatory with downtown LA behind it? Mwaaah! Unless, of course, smog.

The Route – Roll your bike out to Crystal Springs Road and head towards the zoo. "Which way is the zoo?" you ask. Boy, this is going to take a while. You begin pedaling with Interstate 5 on your right and the Carousel on your left. Let's go! Start pedaling!

This is road riding so stay to the right and don't expect the bike lane to be well marked. It comes and goes. But the speed limit is slow so it's not as scary as say, riding on Los Feliz Blvd. That road has White-bicycle-memorial-with-your-name-on-it written all over it.

In 1 mile you will pass the zoo on your left and The Autry Museum on your right. Keep going and at mile 3 you will pass Travel Town on your left. Continue straight. Don't turn right on to Forest Lawn Drive. Here is where the white pipe gate tells cars to suck it. It's bicycle time!

And get ready for 3 ½ miles of steady climbing. Almost 900' of elevation gain. Heading uphill for less than a mile you will turn right at the first intersection. You are now leaving Griffith Park Drive and heading up Mt. Hollywood Drive. There will be no signs. No Signs! Just trust me on the names here.

At mile 5 you will pass the top of Toyon Canyon to your left. This is 2 miles into your climb so you're more than half way up! Another mile and a half – just past the Haunted Picnic Table – you will top out at the intersection with Vista Del Valle Drive coming in on your left. Continue straight noting that we will be returning up Vista Del Valle to close this loop.

We are now 6.5 miles in and the next 2 miles are mostly downhill. When you hit The Griffith Observatory you are back on a live road again. And just like the cars in front of you and behind you, you're cruising through the tunnel. It's super fun.

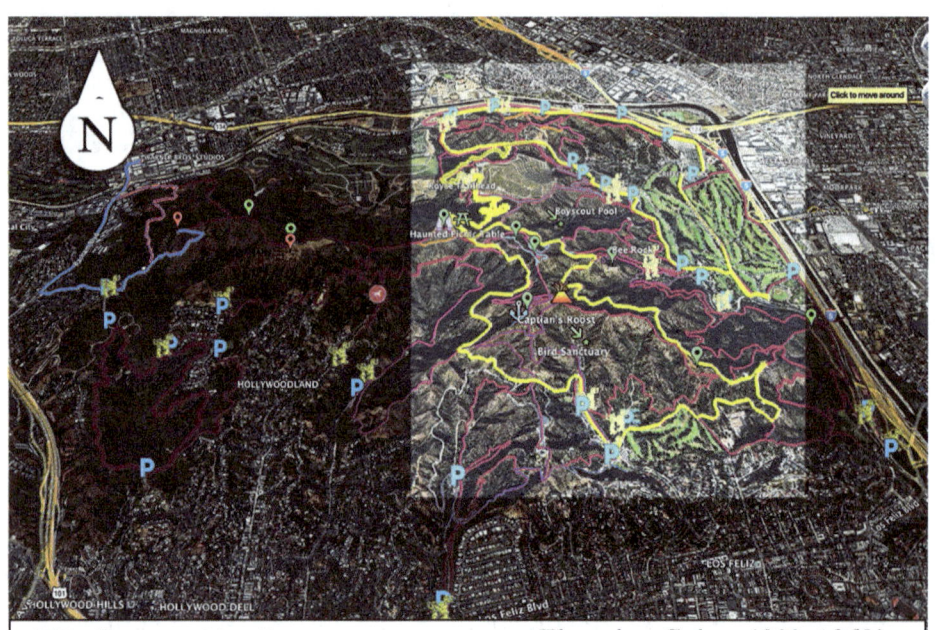

Bike Route - 19 miles
Difficulty -7/10
Parking - Crystal Springs Picnic Area

Elevation Gain - 420' -1360'
Restrooms -Wide variety
Water - Many spots. None Obvious

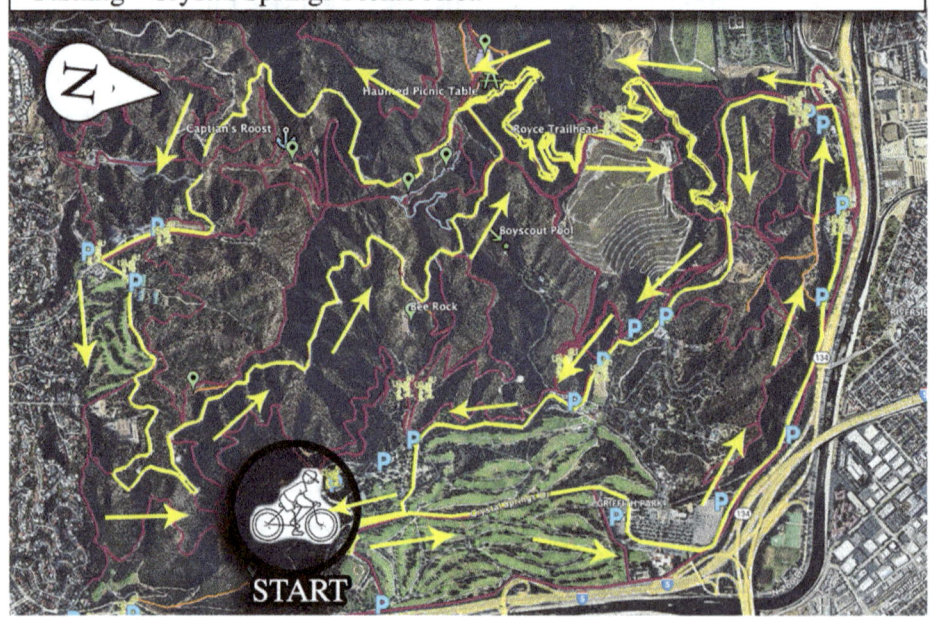

Map data: google earth: image 2024 airbus

When you pass The Greek Theater turn left onto Commonwealth Drive. The Roosevelt Golf Course to your right has a decent snack bar. You are at around 8 ½ miles in so you've earned a break. Grab an overpriced Gatorade or a small box of wine. Whatever your thing is.

Continuing on Commonwealth just past the tennis courts that you will see to your left the white pipe gate stops the cars once again and in about ½ mile we turn left on Vista Del Valle Drive. There will be another white pipe gate because…. Super double bike safety? Not sure. But again, No Signs. Just trust me. It's Vista Del Valle.

Now 1 mile of steady uphill, passing the Joe Klass water stop on your right you will top out at the helipad with it's sweeping 270 degree view. You can see Century City smog all the way to downtown LA smog. From here you have 2 miles of crumbling asphalt overlooking beautiful (?) downtown Glendale.

At mile 12 you will pass Bee Rock on your right and Vista Del Valle gives you one last uphill climb. It's under a mile and tops out at the intersection with Mt. Hollywood Drive I mentioned earlier.

Now it's back downhill the way we came up. It's a fast and furious 2 ½ miles. Try not to fly off the road and into a tree but also…have a blast. At the bottom we hit Griffith Park Drive and turn right. We came in from the left, but we are going back past the golf courses.

FYI we are at about mile 15 ½ right now and we'll see Toyon Canyon to your right. This is where the live car traffic joins you again and bike lane markings on this road are crap but it's fine. It's a slight downhill for 2 miles so you are going to feel like you're getting your second wind. You're not. It's just a very easy section. Sorry for the reality sandwich.

At mile 18 you hit the intersection with Crystal Springs Road. Turn right. Couple hundred feet, turn left. 19 miles. Boom. (Hell yes I rounded up generously. My book, my rules!)

What's the deal with the bike rental shop?

Technically it's called:

Spokes 'N Stuff Bike Rentals
4730 Crystal Springs Dr.
Los Angeles, CA 90027
(323) 653-4099

But in reality it's just a shipping container filled with moderately maintained bicycles that Manny rolls out every Saturday and Sunday kind of by 11:00 am... ish?

Between Memorial Day and Labor day it's kind of open 2:00 pm to 6:00 pm... ish? Think of a Mom and Pop operation and then subtract the mom. Without mom, pop stays up late betting on illegal street fights or something and sometimes sleeps in late so... it opens when it opens.

It's cash only so the guy can't figure out why rentals have been dropping off over the years. Hmmm... But he is gonna at least set up a Vemno account, right? And let the IRS know how many 20's he's pulling in? Nice try, Uncle Sam.

The price is right -$12/hour - but don't plan you day around this place being open when you want it to be.

Eating Places

The Trails – This funky little place is on Fern Dell Drive. It is supposed to be open 8:00 am – 5:00 pm except for Tuesdays however during the week, when things are slow, they just aren't open sometimes. Feels like staffing issues maybe? The menu is heavy on the pastries but they have some sandwich options and some breakfast options. Lots of coffee, tea, and flavored lemonade. It's got more of a Starbucks menu vibe than a sandwich shop menu.

It's cute as a bug and if the line isn't too long and there's a place to sit shoot, get something after your hike. You deserve it…I'm guessing. I don't know you. You might suck.

Griffith Park Café – On Crystal Springs Drive at the Train Rides and where the Pony Rides used to be. (RIP Ponies) This is a classic Roach Coach menu. Burgers, fries, burritos, drinks. Okay, Guy Fieri will never come here and do a TV show about it but, it's got food your kids will love.

Only open on the weekends as of this writing (Oct. 2024) I wouldn't trust that it's open the day you are planning any event. It's run by some City government department so those people don't get bonuses for being good at their job or anything.

Franklin's Market and Café at the Roosevelt Golf Course – It's pretty great! It's attached to the golf course pro shop off of Vermont Ave. It's before you get to the Greek Theater. It has plenty of canned

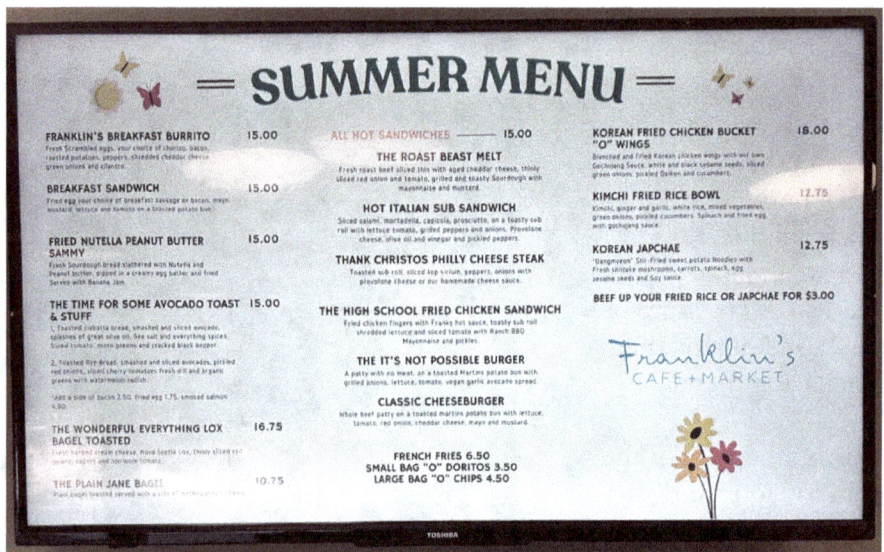

beverages as well as chips and snacks in it's Market section as well as a decent amount of options on the kitchen menu. Open from 7 am to 6 pm. Fun fact… no cash accepted.

Griffith Park Clubhouse – Holy 19th Hole Batman! This little gem is a pretty fancy little spot! At the Wilson & Harding Golf Course on Griffith Park Drive this spot is open 7:00am to 6:30pm every day. You're looking at $15 burgers with a regular sit-down restaurant menu. Beer on tap, full bar. The service is slow when it gets just slightly crowded.

The TV above the bar plays sports like any bar TV should. Sure, one TV has only golf for some reason but the other one plays real sports.

Golf Courses

There are three golf courses in Griffith Park. I haven't golfed in six years because I'm terrible at it and it made me curse more than usual which is already quite a lot. But there are a lot of golfers out there so here are the basics.

Roosevelt Golf Course – 9 holes. Par 4. Right off of Vermont Ave before the Greek Theater. $18 during the week and $26 on the weekends. There are lower rates for Seniors, Juniors, and Twilight golfing. Open 5:30 am to 8:00 pm. Reserve online at golf.lacity.org

Wilson & Harding Golf Courses – both 18 holes and both start at the same clubhouse on Griffith Park Drive near Toyon Canyon. $35 on weekdays and $54 on weekends. Again, there are sliding rates for Seniors, Juniors, & Twilight golfing. Wilson is slightly longer so it might cost and extra buck or two but some say that Harding is more challenging. Open 6:00 AM to 8:30 pm.

Reserve online at golf.lacity.org

Wilson Harding Driving Range – Yeah, it's right there at the same spot. Open from 7:00 am to 9:30 pm. Small bucket is $7 and large is $15.

Epilogue

What an emotional whirlwind folks amiright? The characters, the story arcs, the sweeping locations, the intrigue and drama… I might be exaggerating a bit but you gotta admit, for a trail guide? A pretty freaking fun ride.

Thanks for joining us here at A Run In The Park. If you are holding a paper book in your hand right now A: thanks for buying that and B: remember that we will continue to update the trail videos and website links so when closures or changes are made, we will pass them along. That's why we have the QR codes! Did somebody say "genius?" I will respond to somebody and say, "Thank you."

This is the Griffith Park edition but there are parks all over the country! We hope to be running in your park some day soon!

Jim

www.ingramcontent.com/pod-product-compliance
Lightning Source LLC
LaVergne TN
LVHW021952060526
838201LV00049B/1683